LINGUA LATINA

PER SE ILLUSTRATA

LATINE DOCEO

A Companion for Instructors

Luigi Miraglia
C. G. Brown

LATINE DOCEO

A Companion for Instructors

LINGVA LATINA
PER SE ILLVSTRATA

Pars I:
Familia Romana (1-58510-201-6; hard cover 1-58510-238-5)
Latine Disco: Student's Manual (1-58510-050-1)
Grammatica Latina (1-58510-223-7)
Exercitia Latina I (1-58510-212-1)
Latin-English Vocabulary (1-58510-049-8)
Lingva Latina: Familia Romana CD-ROM for PC (87-90696-08-5)

Pars II:
Roma Aeterna (87-997016-8-5)
Exercitia Latina II (978-1-58510-067-5)
Indices (87-997016-9-3)
Instructions for Part II (1-58510-055-2)
Latin-English Vocabulary (1-58510-052-8)
Lingva Latina: Roma Aeterna CD-ROM For PC (87-90696-09-3)

Ancillaries:
Caesaris: Commentarii De Bello Gallico (87-90696-06-9)
Colloqvia Personarvm (1-58510-156-7)
Menaechmi ex Plavti Comoedia (1-58510-051-X)
P. Vergilii Maronis: Aeneis, Libros I et IV (978-87-90696-17-7)
Petronivs: Cena Trimalchionis (87-90696-04-2)
Plavtus: Amphitryo (87-997016-7-7)
Sallustius & Cicero: Catilina (87-90696-11-5)
Sermones Romani (97-90696-07-7)
Transparency Masters & CD w/ images (Mac/PC) (1-58510-239-3)

Instructor's Materials:
Latine Doceo: Companion for Instructors (1-58510-093-5)
Lingua Latina Set for Instructors: Teacher's Materials & Answer Keys for I&II (1-58510-074-9)

For College Students:
Lingva Latina: A College Companion (978-1-58510-191-7)

For further information on the complete series and new titles, visit www.hackettpublishing.com.

Copyright © Luigi Miraglia and C. G. Brown

ISBN 10: 1-58510-093-5
ISBN 13: 978-1-58510-093-4

Previously published by Focus Publishing/R. Pullins Co.

Focus an imprint of
Hackett Publishing Company, Inc.
P.O. Box 44937
Indianapolis, Indiana

www.hackettpublishing.com

19 18 17 16 15   12 13 14 15

TABLE OF CONTENTS

PREFACE

This guide is addressed to two audiences—the school or university teacher making use of the *LINGVA LATINA PER SE ILLVSTRATA* course in the classroom, and the home-schooling parent guiding his or her child through the course in a program of self-study. The original, Italian-language edition of this book was addressed primarily to the first group, who should have no trouble gleaning what material may be helpful to them from this slender volume, *quantulumcumque est.*

The second group, however, may feel the need for some reassurance as they begin the adventure of *LINGVA LATINA PER SE ILLVSTRATA.* Parents with little or no knowledge of Latin may be intimidated at first by a text composed entirely in Latin. Many suggestions and notes in this guide are directed specifically to them; suggestions addressed to teachers in the classroom can likewise be applied by home-school parents, *mūtātīs mūtāndīs.* Parents should be aware that the *LINGVA LATINA PER SE ILLVSTRATA* course was first conceived as a self-study program, and that Dr. Ørberg to this day teaches the course by correspondence. They will find the course ideally suited for home-schoolers and other students working on their own. There is no reason that even very young students should not be able to work through the course on their own, with guidance from parents who, we hope, may find this manual of some help. They should also rely on the English language student's manual, *LATINE DISCO* which explains the development of the course in clear, simple language.

This guide is very much a work in progress; suggestions, bibliography and corrections are most welcome and can be addressed to brown.2583@osu.edu. Focus Publishing is bringing many new resources to the help of users of the series, not the least of which is the list-serve at http://vlists.net/mailman/listinfo/oerberg For further information on the course or to place book orders one should consult http://www.pullins.com/txt/LinguaLatina.htm

Thanks are due first of all to Dr. Ørberg himself, for his erudition, hospitality, and the incomparable didactic ability which is his hallmark. Thanks to many teachers whose advice reflects their long experience with *LINGVA LATINA PER SE ILLVSTRATA,* including Professors Martha Davis of Temple University, Jeanne Neumann of Davidson College, Boleslav Povsic of Bowling Green University (author of an excellent *Grammatica Latīna*), Ian Thomson of Indiana University (much of whose trailblazing 1975 *Teacher's Guide* has been incorporated into this volume by the author's kind permission), and thanks also to Professor Terence Tunberg of the University of Kentucky's Institute for Latin Studies, whose research into Latin grammatical terminology has been of great help. What errors and mistakes are contained in this book are the sole responsibility of the authors. Special thanks to Ron Pullins of Focus Publishing for his patience and support.

1   cf. Cic., *Dē ōr.,* 1, 4, 15.

Preface to the Italian Edition

No teacher's manual can pretend to be a sacred text, imparting decalogues to instructors as from some Mount Sinai of pedagogy. Nothing is more instructive than experience: *ūsus magister optimus, et ūsus frequēns omnium magistrōrum praecepta superat.*[1] Accordingly, this guide is nothing more than a report, in outline form, on the confirmed experience of teaching the course *LINGVA LATINA PER SE ILLVSTRATA.* Nonetheless, it must be supposed that doubts and uncertainties may arise concerning the correct use of a new instrument such as the text in question. In such moments of uncertainty, as when one voyages through unknown territory, it is always reassuring to have as a companion someone who already knows the place; who knows, through first-hand experience, where the difficult passages are; who has successfully crossed over to what for us is still uncharted territory.

I have used the course of H. H. Ørberg for some years, with exceptional results. Although confident in the abilities of my students, I would never have expected to one day see adolescents capable of reading, correctly and effortlessly, the *Somnium Scīpiōnis* of Cicero. Still less would I have dreamed of hearing teenagers discuss, *in good Latin,* the weighty philosophical questions that text raises. Neverthless, to my great satisfaction, I have been present at such scenes. The happiness of a teacher, nonetheless, is not measured only in terms of knowledge transmitted, but also and above all by the development of an interest and love for the subject. To know that one's own students, *sponte suā* and almost covertly, buy and avidly read the letters to Lucilius, or the *Dē amīcitiā* in the original, or set out in quest of untranslated mediaeval and humanistic texts, gladdens the heart. But to learn that, at the end of their studies, twelve out of twenty Latin students in a high school with a scientific curriculum have chosen to pursue their university careers in departments of literature confirms the teacher's belief that he has not wasted his effort on a useless and barren task. Only a mad love for the humanities, and no abstract pedantry, can make young people oblivious to the banal truism that *litterae nōn dant pānem.*

Therefore this guide, far from wanting to present a collection of precepts and intangible prescriptions, is intended first of all as an *hommage* to Dr. Ørberg, who has made thousands of young people throughout the world perceive Latin, and the tradition of western culture that it transmits, not as a dusty and mouldy monument in some scarcely-frequented museum, but as a living and vital reality whose influence remains powerful in our world, still profoundly rooted in antiquity.

In second place I wanted to present my colleagues with what I have experienced, so as to encourage them to undertake an adventure that will give them only satisfaction. Of course, if someone imagines that with this method he can simply assign homework and exercises so as to then interrogate the victims of the day, he would do better to continue with the conventional translation method. Better still, he should find a new line of work.

Many teachers today are looking for more effective means of instruction, but don't know where to turn. Teachers who love their work, who believe in the value of their efforts, who have not abandoned the audacious project of leading their students to lofty heights, of providing them with the indispensable keys to the edifice of culture, such teachers will find in *LINGVA LATINA PER SE ILLVSTRATA* not, to be sure, a universal panacea to resolve all of their difficulties, but, joined with love for Latin and their students, a most useful instrument for attaining their goal. And so I dedicate this book to my own students at the Liceo Calamandrei in Naples, who thanks to the Ørberg text have made the language of Cicero as it were their own second *sermō patrius*, and now, having learned *sine cortice nāre, ībunt sine mē per undās vītae.*

Luigi Miraglia
Montella
September, 1997

"Nunc enim tē iam exōrēmus necesse est, quoniam retinēs nōs in hōc studiō nec ad aliam dīmittis artem, ut nōbīs explicēs quicquid est istud quod tū in docendō potes… idque ex tē quaerimus (ut nē plūs nōs adsequāmur quam quantulum tū in docendō adsecūtus es) quoniam, quae ā nātūrā expetenda sunt, ea dīcis nōn nimis deesse nōbīs, quid praetereā esse adsūmendum putēs." Tum Crassus adrīdēns: "Quid cēnsēs" inquit "nisi studium et ārdōrem quendam amōris? sine quō cum in vītā nihil quisquam ēgregium, tum certē hoc, quod tū expetis, nēmō umquam adsequētur. Neque vērō vōs ad eam rem videō esse adhortandōs, quōs… nimis etiam flagrāre intellegō cupiditāte. Sed profectō studia nihil prōsunt perveniendī aliquō nisi illud quod eō quō intendās ferat dēdūcatque cognōris. Quārē, quoniam mihi levius quoddam onus impōnitis et ex mē…dē hāc meā, quantulacumque est, facultāte quaeritis, expōnam vōbīs nōn quandam aut perreconditam aut valdē difficilem aut māgnificam aut gravem ratiōnem cōnsuētūdinis meae, quā quondam solitus sum ūtī…."

(*Ex* Cic., *Dē ōr.*, 1, 29,
133-30, 134)

INTRODUCTION BY HANS H. ØRBERG

I am very pleased to have this opportunity to inform Latin teachers and students of my rather unorthodox ideas about Latin teaching. It would perhaps be a good idea to begin by giving you an illustrative example of the way we can all agree that Latin should *not* be taught. I have taken my example from a book by Winston S. Churchill entitled *My Early Life*. Here he tells us how, when seven years old, he was taken to a private boarding school to be taught 'the classics' by the very best teachers. Here is his report:

— I was taken into a Form Room and told to sit at a desk. All the other boys were out of doors, and I was alone with the Form Master. He produced a thin greeny-brown, covered book filled with words in different types of print.

'You have never done any Latin before, have you?' he said.

'No, sir.'

'This is a Latin grammar.' He opened it at a well-thumbed page. 'You must learn this', he said, pointing to a number of words in a frame of lines. 'I will come back in half an hour and see what you know.'

Behold me then on a gloomy evening, with an aching heart, seated in front of the First Declension:

Mensa	a table
Mensa	O table
Mensam	a table
Mensae	of a table
Mensae	to or for a table
Mensa	by, with or from a table

What on earth did it mean? Where was the sense in it? It seemed absolute rigmarole to me. However, there was one thing I could always do: I could learn by heart. And I thereupon proceeded, as far as my private sorrows would allow, to memorise the acrostic-looking task which had been set me.

In due course the Master returned.

'Have you learned it?' he asked.

'I think I can *say* it, sir', I replied; and I gabbled it off.

He seemed so satisfied with this that I was emboldened to ask a question.

'What does it mean, sir?'

'I means what it says. Mensa, a table. Mensa is a noun of the First Declension. There are five declensions. You have learnt the singular of the First Declension.'

'But', I repeated, 'what does it mean?'

'Mensa means a table', he answered.

'The why does mensa also mean O table', I enquired, 'and what does O table mean?'

'Mensa O table is the vocative case', he replied.

'But why O table?' I persisted in genuine curiosity.

'O table, — you would use that in addressing a table, in invoking a table.' And then seeing he was not carrying me with him, 'You would use it in speaking to a table.'

'But I never do', I blurted out in honest amazement.

'If you are impertinent, you will be punished, and punished, let me tell you, very severely', was his conclusive rejoinder.

Such was my first introduction to the classics from which, I have been told, many of our cleverest men have derived so much solace and profit. —

After learning the 1st declension, the next task set poor little Churchill would certainly be to parse and translate sentences like

Scriba poeta est. Puella nautas spectat. Filia reginae cenam parat agricolae.

I know that this sort of inane disconnected sentences have long ago been removed from Latin primers, but even in modern textbooks you may still find ridiculous stories in what is often doubtful Latin, and in any case pupils have to begin by learning grammatical forms and looking up every word in a glossary before they can go on to analyse the parts of a sentence and translate word for word – a procedure that can best be described as "deciphering", not reading.

There is no reason why Latin should be taught by methods totally different from those used in the teaching of modern languages. Latin is a foreign language like other foreign languages and should be taught by similar methods.

Foreign language teachers have always taken a great interest in the process by which a young child acquires a second language when placed in new linguistic surroundings. The speed and accuracy with which a child who has been moved to another country picks up the new language spoken by his or her playfellows and classmates is often quite astonishing; in their limited sphere children may become quite fluent in a new language within a few months. It may be rather a depressing experience for a language teacher to watch the rapid progress of such a child in a foreign language which the teacher's own pupils are very slow in learning. But it must be borne in mind that the teacher is at a great disadvantage being unable to reproduce for the students the ideal situation of the child in a foreign country who is exposed to the foreign language and compelled to communicate in that language from morning to night day in and day out. We have to realize that the "natural" way of learning a foreign language can never be repeated in the classroom.

However, it is worth noticing that there is a great deal of wasted effort especially in the early stages of "natural" language learning, because the learners are exposed to a large number of sentences and words that they do not understand; in fact, at the beginning they do not understand a single word, and only gradually do they begin to make sense of some of the things they hear. There is rather a long passive listening period.

Considering the limited time allowed to the language teacher, something must be done to cut away the passive period and to expose the students from the very start to statements in the foreign language that they understand and no others. One way of doing this is to provide the students with a vocabulary and with rules and explanations about the grammar and structure so as to enable them to translate every sentence into their native language. This is the traditional "grammar-translation" method, by which numerous generations of children have been taught both modern and ancient languages. But this is not nature's way. Children learning their mother tongue or a second language in a foreign country have nobody to translate or to explain grammatical rules, they have to pick up the meaning of words and phrases and the functioning of grammatical forms and structures from what they hear in actual use, directly from linguistic practice, and this does not prevent them from understanding and learning words and structures precisely.

Another way of rationalizing and accelerating the learning process without departing from the direct method followed by nature, is to make every sentence presented to the students immediately intelligible *per se,* or *self-explanatory,* by grading and organizing the introduction of vocabulary and grammar. That means that there is no need to translate or explain grammatical points in the students' own language, they are enabled to discover for themselves directly the meaning of the words and sentences and the functioning of the grammatical rules. This is the teaching procedure to which the term "nature method" or "naturae ratio" has been applied. It represents a rationalization of what may be called the natural learning process. The "nature method" is, to use the words of Alexander Pope, "Nature still, but Nature methodiz'd".

The problem is to "methodize" nature in such a way that there is no waste of time over unintelligible words and sentences, so that every minute of the time at the teacher's disposal is used to teach the students something that they really comprehend and nothing that is beyond them or that they are not supposed to remember. What is needed is an elementary text — in this case a Latin text — that is so organized that the meaning and function of every new word and every new grammatical form or structure, and thus the meaning of every sentence, is made perfectly clear to the students.

How is this possible if nothing is translated or explained in the students' own language? Here again we can learn form observing nature: if children who have to learn a language *secundum naturam* are so quick to grasp the meaning of what is said to them, it is because they are helped by the situation or the *context.* I think the most important lesson a study of "nature" can teach the language teacher is that words and grammatical forms only come to make sense *in context* and therefore should be learned in context.

As a writer of Latin textbooks my task has been to create a variety of contexts or situations in which the words and structures that are to be learned make sense in such a way that the meaning and function of all new words and grammatical forms appear unambiguously from the context in which they occur, or, if necessary, from illustrations or marginal notes using vocabulary already learned. This demands a very carefully graded text. The progressive introduction of words, inflections, and structures, with due regard to their frequency in Latin writers, should conform to a well defined program which not only ensures immediate comprehension, but also assimilation and consolidation owing to the constant recurrence in new surroundings of words and forms already introduced and understood.

This is a purely *inductive* method. Through the observation of a large number of practical examples which form part of a continuous text, the students automatically recognize the meaning of words and sentences, and while familiarizing themselves with the living structure and mechanism of the language they are enabled to work out for themselves, that is to *induce,* the rules of grammar. The text of my Latin course is based on this priciple, which might be called the principle of *contextual induction.*

From the beginning I claimed that the strict observation of this principle need not detract from the readability of the text. In order to hold the attention of the students, to make them *benevolos, attentos, dociles,* they must be offered a text that gives them some kind of relevant information or tells a story that interests them. In fact, if learning from context is to be really effective, the content of the text must help to stimulate interest and curiosity and make it easy for readers to visualize the scenes and situations described and to identify with the characters. Ideally the elementary text should be a connected narrative the content of which captivates the students to such a degree that they look forward to reading the continuation of the story. At the same time, in a Latin course the reading of the text should serve as an introduction to some important aspects of Roman culture.

In the course LINGVA LATINA PER SE ILLVSTRATA I have endeavored to provide an elementary Latin text that combines these qualities with the systematic presentation of vocabulary and grammar that enables the students to understand and learn everything *per se,* from the context alone. This direct method, based on understanding from context, or *contextual induction,* is, I believe, more efficient and rewarding than the traditional grammar-translation method. The decisive factor is the satisfaction felt by the students when they discover that they can find out the meaning of everything on their own without having to look up words in vocabularies or rules and paradigms in grammars: they can actually understand the Latin passage that is put before them or that the teacher reads aloud to them. This comes as a pleasant surprise to the students, especially if they find that the text really makes sense, that there is an exciting story to follow and that they learn interesting facts about the ancient Romans, not least the fact that they are truly human beings like the students themselves.

The direct understanding from context gives the students self-confidence and stimulates concentration. It sharpens their faculties of observation and reasoning, faculties that will be greatly needed as the sentences grow more complex. Reading in this way they move on step by step towards the ultimate object of Latin teaching: the reading of Latin literature in Latin with real understanding and appreciation.

Hans H. Ørberg

PROLEGOMENA TO TEACHING
LINGVA LATINA PER SE ILLVSTRATA

A milestone in Latin teaching

If western literature derives ultimately from the Greeks, it is through Latin letters that this tradition was brought to a new perfection and transmitted to the west. With the spread of western civilization through the whole world, the riches of Latin literature have a universal relevance. And since no translation of Latin works into modern languages can fully render the original text, it is lamentable that today the knowledge of Latin has fallen to such a point that otherwise educated people can barely understand this language or are altogether ignorant of it. Faced with such circumstances, it seems opportune to rededicate our forces to the diffusion of Latin in our schools.

Since reaching a nadir in the late 1970s Latin enrollments have been steadily rising in American schools. A host of utilitarian arguments—improved SAT scores, AP credits, college admissions prospects—have helped attract a new generation of Latin students. There is currently a shortage of qualified Latin teachers, and the danger exists that a lack of qualified teachers may stifle the burgeoning interest in Latin. While utilitarian arguments may indeed be useful, ultimately the case for Latin teaching must be based on the importance of the subject, and this case in turn cannot be made be made effectively unless the language is well taught. If after several years of study students are unable to understand correctly and without help of a vocabulary even a few lines of elementary Latin, if, even worse, their experience gives them an aversion to Latin, then the current renewal of interest in Latin is destined to be shortlived.

When students cannot read Latin texts *fluently*, we cannot hope to achieve the goal which not only justifies, but in our opinion renders indispensable the study of Latin in any curriculum that aims to provide the tools of a solid cultural formation. This goal is not merely to acquire the rudiments and a vague "cultural literacy" but rather to give students access to the sources of our literary, scientific, juridic, historical, theological and philosophical traditions—not only to the works of antiquity but also to those of the middle ages, the Renaissance, and modern times, written in the language which has been the vehicle of western culture. It is an enormous and extraordinary collection of treasures closed in vaults and safes the only key to which is possession of the *lingua Urbis et orbis*.

For the attainment of this goal, in the nineteen-fifties scholars from all over the world (some of whose prefaces may be found in Appendix III) looked for the best approach to the teaching of Latin. No method seemed more effective than the pedagogy already applied with success to the teaching of modern languages. The quarrel is of course still underway, but the reasons that are normally adduced against this method of approaching Latin (and, we might add, Greek) are for the most part groundless pretexts.

It is said, for example, that the pedagogy of modern languages has as its goal communication, that students of Spanish, French, and German have to learn to speak those languages, while students of ancient languages have as their sole objective that of gaining access to ancient texts. As anyone can observe in our higher institutions of learning, this prejudice lacks foundation. Students begin with communicative and colloquial contexts — generally more accessible, because paratactic — and, after some time, are capable of reading the classical texts: from Cervantes to Borges in Spanish, from Montaigne to Camus for French, from Wolfram von Eschenbach to Goethe and Heine for German. But, as every teacher of foreign languages can confirm, "the simultaneous learning of listening, speaking, writing and reading is very important in language learning. But particularly it is the productive aspects of the language — speaking and writing — that are essential in mastering the receptive aspects of listening and reading. A student cannot have a clear idea of a sentence he hears or reads unless it is a sentence for which he has the grammatical competence which underlies its production... If a student wants reading power, he must have active control over what he reads... The only effective way to attain the goal of a 'reading knowledge' of a language is to gain an active mastery of the productive aspects of that language."[2] The true difference between the teaching of modern languages and that of the ancient languages consists in the fact that the former see in the mastery of the spoken language also a direct end, while for the latter writing and speaking are primarily means for achieving a deeper and more complete comprehension of written texts.

One might ask whether the structure of Latin allows the creation of texts (as has been done for modern languages) that would be immediately comprehensible — without the help of a translation — even by those who don't know a single word of Latin. Arthur M. Jensen, author of an English course "according to the natural method," in which he applied this didactic method, did not doubt that it could also be applied to Latin. This confidence was shared by Hans Henning Ørberg, a young Latinist who committed himself to the undertaking. Thus was born the present course *LINGVA LATINA PER SE ILLVSTRATA*. Distinguished philologists from various countries verified the correctness of Latin style, and still others expressed their own opinion of the method with the prefaces published in this manual. Over half a century the author, gifted with an exceptional sensibility and didactic genius, welcoming the criticisms and suggestions of teachers and students, has continuously perfected the course with successive editions up to the present time. It is currently taught in all regions of the *orbis terrārum,* in China and elsewhere in Asia, Australia, Africa,

---

2   pp. 75-76 in Diller, K.C. 1971. *Generative Grammar, Structural Linguistics, and Language Teaching*, Rowley, Mass: Newbury House.

Europe and the Americas; the international success of his method over fifty years is proof of its efficacy.

The course is constructed in such a way that the meaning and function of each new word emerges clearly from the context, and every word is repeated with sufficient frequency to impress itself in the memory. Dr. Ørberg calls this approach "contextual induction." To facilitate more rapid and profitable reading, care has been taken that in every chapter the new words introduced be in a proportion no greater than one to every 25-30 words already learned. Nevertheless, by the end of the course the careful student will have assimilated over 3,500 words, constituting (according to frequency studies of Latin words) practically all the vocabulary of common use. With this lexical foundation, the student will be able to read most works of Latin literature with relative ease.[3]

Grammar is likewise assimilated through the readings by contextual induction. The presentation of rules is avoided until the students have encountered examples of them in situations, and can thus understand the principles on the basis of their application.[4] This inductive approach is complemented by the use of paradigms and grammatical analysis. Each chapter also includes a section, entitled *Grammatica Latina*, which presents, in Latin, a clear explanation of grammatical phenomena adequate to the current level of the student. *LATINE DISCO* provides further grammatical explanation in English. The reference grammar *SYNTAXIS LATINA*[5] functions as a complement to *FAMILIA ROMANA*, and contains an ordered description of the fundamental syntactical structures in English, with examples taken from Ørberg's texts; it will prove useful when the instructor or student wishes to develop a topic, or find a grammatical overview.

An important factor in the growth of Latin studies in American schools has been the emergence of new textbooks that have emulated Ørberg's approach. These books have up to now been more widely used than *LINGVA LATINA PER SE ILLVSTRATA* in part because they seem more accessible to some teachers, and partly for marketing reasons. While representing an advance over grammar/translation textbooks, these courses are manifestly the work of a committee, where *LINGVA LATINA PER SE ILLVSTRATA* is that of a pedagogical genius. This is apparent from the quality of Latin in these texts, which often seems artificial by comparison with that of *LINGVA LATINA PER SE ILLVSTRATA*. Most importantly, none of those three courses achieve the seamless transition from the authors' Latin to that of classical writers that is the hallmark of the Ørberg course. For example, the jump from *Ecce IIB* to *Ecce III* is considerable; students find the original texts of Caesar much more difficult than what they have previously encountered. By contrast, when students read unadapted passages from ancient authors in *LINGVA LATINA PER SE ILLVSTRATA* they often have the impression that they are even easier than the Ørberg Latin they have been reading without difficulty. This because they have been well-prepared by the meticulous and almost invisible gradations in Ørberg's work— *ars latet arte sua!*

The quantity of long vowels is always marked, so that the student can distinguish longs from shorts and develop the good

pronunciation helpful in assimilating vocabulary and necessary for reading Latin poetry. It is up to the instructor whether to adopt the so-called pronunciation *restitūta* for which the immediate recognition of long vowels is indispensible, or the late Latin pronunciation Even students using the latter pronunciation, however, will find that distinguishing long from short vowels is essential to correct accentuation and often even to comprehension.

GENERAL METHODOLOGICAL PRINCIPLES

The goal: fluent reading of the classics

Serious and consistent study of the *LINGVA LATINA PER SE ILLVSTRATA* course yields a mastery of all the fundamental morphological, syntactic and lexical structures of the language of Rome, soon culminating — much earlier than by any other system — in the *correct reading* of the classical texts. We distinguish *correct reading* from translation. The difficult task of translation presupposes the ability to understand the text directly (without vocabularies and ponderous grammars) in the target language. Correct reading makes translation, as Martinet defines it, a "phrasal reformulation," and not, as too often happens, an improbable labor of decoding an incomprehensible text: a task that may resemble more a game of charades and chance than a true translation, with dubious pedagogical results.

A good beginning

Dīmidium factī qui coepit habet. A successful outcome depends on a good beginning, setting out immediately on the right path, a path that diverges from the received methods in not a few points, and which therefore may now and then create practical difficulties for teachers used to the conventional procedures. To that end, we should like to furnish some methodological help and direction. This introductory manual is intended as a guide, and not as some code from which it is forbidden to diverge—teachers are obviously free to modify, adapt, select, and revise it according to their needs, inclinations, and situation. Nevertheless, the instructor should keep in mind that a course such as this one functions at its best if used according to the author's intentions, and that accordingly every innovation, detour, or variation ought to be harmonious with the goals of the text. We therefore ask the teacher or home-schooling parent to give this manual the time necessary for an attentive reading. The didactic experience of the reader will then suggest how to best put into practice the different precepts presented here, and will probably lead each teacher to develop new and personal ways of presenting the material. It nevertheless seems indispensable to assimilate some basic points of methodology, so that elements different from, or even contrary to, the principles and overall structure on which the course is based do not pervert its nature, producing a didactic hybrid with disappointing results.

Communicate enthusiasm for the subject: the importance of Latin

It is essential that, from the very first day, students feel the desire to undertake this new and fascinating study, and to gain the greatest profit from it. It is therefore obvious that the teacher's first task is to infect students with an enthusiasm for what they are going to learn, for the possibilities Latin will afford them, for the ever-broadening horizons it will open before them. The goal

---

3   Cf. Lodge, G. 1907. *The Vocabulary of High School Latin.* New York: Teachers College.

4   Lado, R. 1964. *Language Teaching: A Scientific Approach.*

5   Forthcoming from Focus Publishing.

of our journey should be clear from the first day—the students should see that the knowledge of Latin will be to their great personal and intellectual enrichment. The teacher must emphasize that the study of Latin is an indispensable means of acquiring a living knowledge of the culture of ancient Rome, the foundation of western civilization. The life and ideals of the Romans, the millennial history of the empire, the literature and art which assimilated and elaborated the treasures of Greek culture—this is the spiritual heritage of one of the most glorious ages of human history, a heritage which still today leaves its indelible imprint on our world. Latin, the language of this civilization, has therefore a singular importance, and it is not surprising if in the course of the centuries this language has been more studied than any other.

Beyond the utilitarian arguments

No nation today has Latin as its mother tongue; this is what is meant when Latin is spoken of as a "dead language." But such an expression can give rise to misunderstandings. Young people are ill-disposed to give their efforts to the study of a dead subject, and even more so in an age of pragmatism when every object is evaluated in terms of its practical utility. A contemporary mental deformation inclines us—and the young are especially susceptible to this banal manner of thinking—to scorn whatever does not manifest some convenience or advantage *īlicō et immediātē*. Students accustomed to immediate stimulation by television, the internet, and habits of consumption may regard anything demanding sustained effort for its acquisition with suspicion and disgust. Here, at this initial juncture, the ability of the teacher is decisive. The good teacher should be able to separate students from this perverse vision of things. The teacher must convince that, although the development of virtue, the life of the soul, the arts, music, and poetry have no immediate practical utility, they are nonetheless of the greatest advantage and deserve to be pursued with all our strength. In this first presentation of the value of Latin studies it will be necessary to underline that for centuries Latin was the living language of the Roman empire, just as English is a living language for us today. This so-called "dead language" was not only living, but vital enough to survive the fall of the empire and to serve throughout the middle-ages and modern times as the language of culture in the West.

Latin: a "dead language"?

In this regard the teacher may wish to read the article by Professor Tunberg in Appendix V, entitled "*Latinitas:* The misdiagnosis of Latin's rigor mortis." This article suggests the range and value of Latin as both a language of culture and a pragmatic means of communication throughout the centuries of our western tradition. Students should be made aware of the bimillenial heritage of Latin literature. A visit to a university library will allow students to recognize how much cultural production into the early twentieth century was written in Latin, works which have never been translated into modern languages. Visits to art galleries, museums, universities, churches, and monuments, a slide presentation of same, or even inspection of our currency can show the uninterrupted use of the language of western culture. Students will be interested to see how the use of a single language created the sense of an international *rēs pūblica litterāria et philosophica*, both synchronic and diachronic, which includes all those who for centuries have labored to transmit the wisdom of antiquity, *veterum sapientia,* and of which they too can be a part.

A vital language

Awareness of the value of a unifying language is second nature to our American students, who take for granted the universality of English. A comparison between Latin and English as *Weltsprachen*—international languages—provides an opportunity for historical and even philosophical reflection. Contemporary English almost dispenses with syntax, preferring parataxis and short sentences. Modern languages in general manifest "the expansion of the role played by the noun with a corresponding diminution of that of the verb,"[6] a standardization of the means of expression. A meager form of expression, directed towards pragmatic and commercial exchanges, repudiates the demand for nuance and precision characteristic of the language of culture and civilization, heir to an ancient wisdom arduously won. The reduction of Latin to the role of a dead language, even in the field of culture, reflects the desire for a separation of scientific research from humanistic knowledge. Positivism and naturalism have played a leading role in this process, and the myth of continuous and unending "progress," inaugurated in the Enlightenment and still persistent, like some collective archetype, as an ineradicable *īdōlum forī*, has for many relegated the patrimony of the ancients to the realm of useless fairy tales and empty abstractions easily dispensed with. This myth represents the victory of incessant becoming over transcendental Being, of the world of unstable and contingent *doxa* over the luminosity of *alétheia*.[7] Its outcome has often been the replacement of spiritual aspirations with the mean striving for material prosperity, the only goal apparent for those who experience existence as a *sistere sē ex nihilō*, doomed *revertī in nihilum.*

Such a historical perspective can be communicated to youngsters in a lively and natural way, without the burden of concepts disproportionate to their age. To communicate enthusiasm it is necessary that we ourselves be convinced of the formative value of Latin, and that we fascinate our students with this passion as if by a contagion: *nēmō dat quod nōn habet.* The success of any didactic enterprise depends on the teacher's belief, not only in the efficacy of the method undertaken, but also in the extraordinary value of the subject, of the fundamental task of transmitting that discipline to new generations, that historical memory not fall into oblivion.

Students should be made aware that Latin was the international language of science until the beginning of the nineteenth century, and that the nomenclature of science, in particular of medicine, zoology, and botany, is for the most part Latin. In most European universities one cannot enroll in courses of biology, natural science, or medicine without passing a Latin exam, as was the case in American medical schools not so long ago. Latin is still the official language of the Catholic Church, in which encyclicals, bulls, and documents are written. Countless Latin expressions are used in everyday speech—a proposal is rejected *ā priōrī*, an honor is conferred *mōtū propriō*, a war is waged to restore the *status quō,* a person is described as *suī generis.*

6   Biagi, M. Luisa Altieri. 1984. I gerghi della scienza contemporanea, in: *Letteratura e scienza, a cura di A. Battistini.* Bologna: Zanichelli.

7   Romano Amerio relates this renaissance of Pyrrhonism (skepticism) to mobilism, the belief that the only permanence is change. Amerio, Romano. 1996. Iota Unum., Kansas City: Sarto House.

The importance of Latin for knowledge of English

The importance of Latin for English vocabulary can easily be illustrated through sample etymologies. English conserves many Latin words that do not exist even in Italian, such as *perfunctory, despicable,* derived respectively from *perfungī, dēspicere;* words such as *herb, theater, triumph,* and *human* are almost identical with their Latin ancestors—*herba, theātrum, triumphus, hūmānus.* If students are taught how the Norman invasion of 1066 and the subsequent intercourse of Anglo-Saxon with the neo-Latin dialect called French gave birth to English, they will understand why over half of our vocabulary derives from Latin.

The key to learning foreign languages

The teacher should emphasize that Latin is the key to learning foreign languages. This is most obvious in the case of the Romance languages developed in Spain, France, Italy, Portugal, etc. When in these countries Latin was supplanted by its modern dialects in everyday speech, it nonetheless remained uncontested as the language of culture, and thus continued to enrich the vernacular languages. In Italian, for example, although words such as *oro, agosto* and *vino* are simply the Latin words *aurum, Augustus* and *vīnum* which were always spoken and transformed through a natural development, many others were taken from Latin after having been abandoned for many centuries, or having survived only in educated circles—words such as *aureo, augusto, vinicolo.* It is no exaggeration to say that one must learn Latin to know the Romance languages well.

Not just a gateway to the Romance languages, the study of Latin opens the door to an understanding of the nature of language itself. Many students will have no practical understanding of English grammar until they study Latin. Student should be led to reflect on the connection of thought to language, and recognize that their mastery of a syntactically more sophisticated language than our own will discipline and develop their intelligence. Here the words of the great twentieth-century Latinist, Ugo Enrico Paoli, are pertinent: "To put the learning of a modern language on the same level as the study of Latin is to ignore the particular value of Latin as a propaedeutic to the study of any other language, since it furnishes a model of the method to follow in learning a language, whatever it may be. In studying a modern language, whoever has studied Latin with normal progress will find himself at an incalculable advantage over someone who knows nothing of Latin. Of course this argument will have no weight with those who would obstinately deny it. But not everything can be denied. We see, for example, that our university students of literature who have learned Latin in high school succeed with little difficulty, and waste little time in understanding, for example, a German text, even if they have never studied German in school... This aptitude for rapidly finding one's bearings in the study of a living language, whence does it derive if not from having studied Latin?"[8]

Confronting students's prejudices

All the same, even if students are well aware of the advantages of the study of Latin, they may begin their studies with some skepticism about their prospects of success. This is perfectly comprehensible, given the widespread belief that Latin is a hard nut to crack, reserved to an intellectual elite and inaccessible to those who lack some special aptitude for languages. Students may already have been influenced by their older siblings or friends who, tormented by abstruse grammatical rigmarole and linguistic pedantry, become propagators of the idea that Latin is a useless undertaking, not to be mastered in a lifetime. It is essential to attack this fundamental prejudice, and demonstrate its falsehood.

Everyone can learn Latin

Most students begin their Latin studies between twelve and fourteen years old, enthusiastically beginning their entry into a new world. This childish enthusiasm can be directed towards their studies if only their teacher can convince them that Latin offers them the keys to this world. Incite their enthusiasm: make it clear from the first day that they are not only studying abstract grammatical rules, but texts and a living language. Reassure them that they will understand everything, that Latin will be easy for them, that they will even succeed in speaking correctly. The success that the students will predictably achieve through the *LINGVA LATINA PER SE ILLVSTRATA* course will be a confirmation of these promises from the outset. Explain to them that students in our schools unfortunately often do not learn Latin well and thus learn to hate it, because the methods generally used are ill-adapted for learning a language and thus put their abilities and patience through an unnecessary ordeal. Underline for them the novelty of the tool at their disposal, widely recognized as an ideal instrument for learning the language well and without wasted effort. Above all, reassure them that they will succeed in their project, because they are setting out on a rational course.

It is to be stressed that any normal person can learn Latin. They can expect to succeed without slogging away at grammars and vocabularies, without losing themselves in the labyrinth of logical analyses and translations, without having to memorize countless grammatical rules and their relative exceptions. They can immediately begin to read and understand Latin. This does not mean that they need not study grammar, and indeed become masters of it—the fundamental point is whether grammar is a function of language, or language of grammar. It might be called a Copernican revolution in teaching, but it in fact marks a return to the methods used before nineteenth century scientific models made of Latin not so much a language as an exercise in translation and analysis.

Advantages of the Ørberg method

This indeed is the secret of the *LINGVA LATINA PER SE ILLVSTRATA* course. The text is constructed in such a way that all words and new grammatical forms are clear from the ensemble of the story. Thus the torture of continual page-turning in dictionaries and grammars is avoided, replaced by the satisfaction of resolving difficulties oneself, with one's own intelligence. And since the text that the students are reading is both instructive and enjoyable, learning Latin becomes a work that is attractive, or even fascinating.

Students and teachers must make a commitment

Fascinating work, but work all the same. Students should not be led to believe that they can learn Latin in their sleep, or without any effort. Nothing is gained by indolence. To follow the course to proper advantage requires good-will and energy, from the

---

8   Paoli, U.E. 1959. Latino sì o latino no?, in: *L'osservatore politico e letterario* .

student as much as from the teacher. It will be necessary to work on the texts with perseverance and continuity, if possible every day. But when will and interest are not lacking, work becomes a pleasure and is doubly effective. If they persevere, the students can expect to learn also this most important lesson.

By the same token, this course is not recommended for teachers and home-school parents who want to expend the minimum possible energy in their task. Those who are by training or temperament wedded to a passive approach to Latin study quite likely will not teach these books effectively. The rewards the *LINGUA LATINA* course can offer will be commensurate with the instructor's level of engagement. Effective use of the text in the classroom requires a close and active knowledge of the material, and the desire to improve one's own command of the language.

STRUCTURE OF THE COURSE

The books

The basic text of the *LINGVA LATINA PER SE ILLVSTRATA* series is the volume *FAMILIA ROMANA*. Necessary supplements are the English language student's manual, *LATINE DISCO*, and the workbook *EXERCITIA LATINA*. Also useful is the volume *COLLOQUIA PERSONARUM*, which presents dialogues keyed to the first twenty-four chapters of *FAMILIA ROMANA*. The slender volume *GRAMMATICA LATINA* supplies a complete morphology and a useful list of verbal principal parts, complementing the tables and index in the back of *FAMILIA ROMANA*. The *index vocabulōrum* in the back of *FAMILIA ROMANA* lists words by their first appearance with a given meaning; this makes it possible for students to recur to the original context of a word's appearance to recall its meaning. On completing the thirty-five chapters of *FAMILIA ROMANA* students have learned the basics of Latin syntax and morphology. They are then ready to read Ørberg's edition of Plautus's *Amphitrō, Caesar's Bellum Gallicum,* or *Sermōnēs Rōmānī,* or they can proceed directly to the second volume of the text, *ROMA AETERNA*, which includes chapters 36-56 of the course. *ROMA AETERNA* has its own English language student's manual and accompanying volumes of *EXERCITIA LATINA*. A comprehensive booklet of *INDICES* to the whole course includes all words in the course, an analytical index of proper names in the two volumes, lists of the *Fastī consulārēs* and *triumphālēs* and a list of form changes (such as *tul-* and *lāt-* from *fer.*)

A Latin novel

The two volumes *FAMILIA ROMANA* and *ROMA AETERNA* compose a work of more than 700 pages divided into 56 chapters. It is a coherent narrative, a kind of novel. Written completely and exclusively in Latin, it can nevertheless be read from the first to the last page by someone who is completely ignorant of Latin at the outset.

From the first chapters of the course it is apparent that one is not dealing with a dry text composed with the unique purpose of illustrating grammatical rules. The plot and personalities have a lively development, involving the students and provoking their interest as the reading continues. This aspect of the course is fundamental: the course material has been developed in such a way that the interest of the subject and the plot will renew the student's dedication to learning the language so as to arrive all the more

quickly and effectively at the goal of mastery. At the same time, the student will not have the feeling of reading a text constructed with the sole goal of learning and practicing grammatical rules. Furthermore, the student will be attentive to the character and the behavior of the personalities that animate the story, the cultural background of the Roman world, and will thus better penetrate the genius of the language—the *indolēs sermonis*. Appendix IV to this volume presents a basic bibliography on aspects of Roman civilization broached in this course; some teachers may want to use these secondary materials to elaborate on these subjects in the classroom.

The first chapter gives a geographical orientation to the Roman world. It is an introduction, and does not yet enter *in mediās rēs*. Then students meet a Roman family, whose daily life will be developed in the succeeding chapters through some dramatic vicissitudes. They will encounter the habits and customs of the Romans; they will relive pages from history and legend, of pagan mythology and nascent Christianity. They will accompany a fugitive slave and his betrothed on a perilous navigation, follow a Roman legion on campaign in Germany, and take part in the ceremonies and banquets of a world far removed from our own. In short, they will live day by day the life of ancient Rome. And through this experience of the ancient world they will arrive, on their own and with the help of their teacher, at the ability to read and understand Latin literature—Livy, Nepos, Sallust, and Cicero. If the text is used correctly even texts traditionally considered difficult will be read with ease.

The pictures

The maps and illustrations by Peer Lauritzen make up an integral part of the course. Costumes, objects of common use, public and private buildings, furniture, etc, have all been reconstructed with fidelity to the literary and archaeological evidence.[9] But the task of the pictures is not only to provide a lively illustration of the atmosphere, people, and situations described in the text. The images are also a precious tool for learning Latin. They are usually accompanied by a phrase in Latin—making the picture speak in Latin, as it were, giving a precise and lively sense to the Latin words. Thus the students see that which is described and assimilate Latin as a living language. Comenius, the sixteenth century pedagogue, wrote the following in the preface to his *"Orbis sēnsuālium pictus"*: *"Sēnsūs... obiecta sua semper quaerunt, absentibus illīs hebēscunt, taediōque suī hūc illūc sē vertunt; praesentibus autem obiectīs suīs hilarēscunt, vīvēscunt, et sē illīs affīgī, dōnec rēs satis perspecta sit, libenter patiuntur. Libellus ergō hic ingeniīs... captīvandīs et ad altiōra studia praeparandīs bonam nāvābit operam"*[10]. These words may also serve as a preface to the methodology of the course *LINGVA LATINA PER SE ILLVSTRATA.*

---

9   Overhead transparency masters illustrating the models for some of these drawings are available from Focus Publishing.

10   I. A. Comenius, *Orbis sēnsuālium pictus: hoc est omnium fundāmentālium in mundō rērum et in vītā āctiōnum pictūra et nōmenclātūra,* facsimile of the third London edition of 1672 w. introduction by James Bowen, Sydney University Press, 1967. See J.A. Komensky, *Opera omnia,* vol 17, Academia Praha, Pragae 1970, pp. 59-60.

The student's manual: LATINE DISCO

The student's manual presents a commentary on the text of *FAMILIA ROMANA* in English, providing an orientation to each chapter and drawing attention to certain points of special importance. These instructions are also useful to the teacher or home-schooling parent, because they contain all the fundamental grammatical points covered in each chapter. Nevertheless, we recommend that students not read these instructions before they have minutely studied the corresponding chapter, for the simple reason that students should be able to understand the text on their own, and will better assimilate the material by doing so. The manual will then serve the student as a review and confirmation. It may also be helpful to students who need to catch up with the class after a prolonged absence.The instructions are written in simple and clear language, with summaries and outlines in the margins which facilitate the memorization of basic points of syntax and morphology. After incorporating these points into his explanation of each chapter the teacher may then advise students to make a careful study of the instructions in *LATINE DISCO*.

EXERCITIA LATINA

The volume of exercises is an indispensable counterpart to *FAMILIA ROMANA*. It contains more than 400 exercises for the reinforcement of morphology, syntax, and vocabulary and to evaluate, through questions in Latin, comprehension of the text that has been read. The *exercitia,* like each chapter of *FAMILIA ROMANA,* are normally divided into three *lēctiōnēs*. The beginning of each *lēctiō* is indicated in *FAMILIA ROMANA* by a Roman numeral in the margin (e.g. in chapter one the first *lēctiō* is from lines 1-21, the second from lines 22-61, etc.) These exercises are of the greatest importance for giving students a full command of linguistic structures, and should all be completed. While the complete texts of *FAMILIA ROMANA* and *ROMA AETERNA* should as a rule be read out loud expressively by both teacher and students and studied in class, we are inclined to suggest that the *exercitia* generally be assigned as homework. While most learning should be done in class under the direction of the teacher, it is undeniable that students have to do some exercise and assimilation on their own. Like all such "rules" this should be taken *cum grānō salis,* and it may sometimes be opportune, especially at the early stages of the course, to do the exercises in class. In any case all the exercises should normally be corrected in class by the teacher, whether individually or with the class as a whole.

COLLOQUIA PERSONARUM

The twenty-four *COLLOQUIA PERSONARUM* correspond to the chapters of *FAMILIA ROMANA: capitulum prīmum/colloquium prīmum, capitulum secundum/collo-quium secundum,* etc. The goal of the *colloquia* is to repeat the vocabulary and grammatical structures encountered in the chapter in a different context. Their dialogical structure lends itself to dramatization. Such representations could even be combined at the end of the year to make up a theatrical presentation. This kind of work has an enormous value for learning vocabulary and transforming grammatical structures into reflexes. Since the dialogues include a small number of characters they can also be enacted by home-school students and their parents.

GRAMMATICA LATINA

This handbook describes the parts of speech and gives a systematic presentation of all the forms students must commit to memory in the course of their work with *LINGUA LATINA PER SE ILLUSTRATA*. Once entire paradigms have been encountered teachers may find it helpful to assign morphological synopses on a regular basis until all forms have been thoroughly assimilated—a sample verb synopsis sheet is included as Appendix VIII. Particularly useful is the list of irregular principal parts on pp. 23-26 of *GRAMMATICA LATINA;* by the end of the course students should have all these forms thoroughly memorized. At an intermediate stage teachers may find helpful the list of principal parts of the fifty most common Latin verbs, presented in the more conventional order, in Appendix VI. Students should know all of these principal parts by heart on completing *FAMILIA ROMANA*.

This reference manual attests that the *LINGVA LATINA PER SE ILLVSTRATA* course in no way prescinds from teaching the grammar, declensions and conjugations that confront students on the very first pages of grammar/translation textbooks. The criticism of the grammar/translation approach implicit in *LINGVA LATINA PER SE ILLVSTRATA* is not that it describes Latin syntax with insufficient clarity. The problem consists in determining whether, in particular for children and adolescents—but not only for them—the systematic learning of this scientific description is the best way of learning the language, of mastering the rules that govern its function not only in such a way as to be able to express them abstractly, but to convert them *in sūcum et sanguinem,* so that they become automatic reflexes making possible, without further reflection, a fluent reading of the text with full comprehension. *LINGVA LATINA PER SE ILLVSTRATA* teaches grammar and morphology all the more effectively by reversing the order of presentation so that *usus* precedes *doctrīna*. The grammatical rule is *first* encountered in the text and inductively understood from its context, and *then* it is systematically ordered and schematized. The memorization of paradigms is simplified through the prior recognition of forms in context. Thus both *GRAMMATICA LATINA* and the *SYNTAXIS LATINA*[11] serve as works to be consulted once teacher and students have arrived at the last treatment of an argument, so as to then definitively establish the forms and rules in the mind. In most cases this involves nothing more than a deeper treatment of subjects already encountered in the text itself or in the student's manual. If our goal is not for our students to acquire information *about* the Latin language, without knowing how to *use* the language even in its receptive aspects (reading and comprehension), we must avoid beginning with the rule as a prescriptive norm and then looking for its application in texts and exercises. We must on the contrary bring to an ever greater degree of awareness that which has already been assimilated and understood in usage.

Pious reticence at the first stage of teaching grammar

As far as the explanation of syntactical rules is concerned, it is best to always keep in mind the didactic principle of pious reticence. An excessive accumulation of abstract concepts presented at the same time is not conducive to their assimilation. It is thus necessary to present such material drop by drop, as it were,

---

11   Forthcoming from Focus Publishing.

through successive approximations, as when making a mosaic one begins with the most important pieces and then works towards the periphery.

For example, in explaining constructions with the verb *iubēre* it is conventional to say that (1) *iubēre* takes an accusative/infinitive construction: *Caesar iubet mīlitēs rescindere pontem*; (2) that, if the person commanded is not expressed, the passive infinitive is used: *Caesar iubet pontem rescindī*; (3) that the verb becomes personal in the passive voice: *mīlitēs iussī sunt rescindere pontem;* (4) that, especially in juridical language and when decrees of the people or magistrates are spoken of, the verb is often used with *ut* + subjunctive, by analogy with *imperāre*: *senātus iussit, ut iūra servārentur reī pūblicae*; (5) that the verbs *vetāre, sinere, prohibēre*, etc. govern the same constructions. Can one reasonably suppose that a student can keep all these rules in mind and sufficiently practice their use? This is but one example, and not the worst. How then to proceed? When the verb is first encountered, students should be made to reflect on the fact that *iubēre* governs an accusative with infinitive, and the teacher should show the fortitude to pass over the rest in silence, for the time being. Certainly this is not the whole truth. Or better, it is not a complete treatment of the constructions of *iubēre*. But it is preferable to momentarily pass over a part of the truth in silence, rather than risking that no trace of that which we have wanted to communicate should remain after several days, or that in any case an insurmountable gulf be created between linguistic practice and the abstractly formulated "rule." Thus it suffices to observe that *iubēre* governs the accusative and infinitive, and even this observation should not be made *sīc et simpliciter* by the teacher, until the students have first figured out for themselves that in the accusative/infinitive construction in general a phrase like *Iūlius servum suum Tūsculum īre iubet* (XI. 44-45) can mean "Julius orders his slave to go to Tusculum." From this point on students will have many occasions to meet and apply this syntactical "rule" until it becomes spontaneous and natural, on having encountering the verb *iubēre,* to look for the accompanying accusative and infinitive. They will thus have transformed a grammatical rule into a permanent possession, so that encountering any other construction will seem strange to them. Then, and only then, should one add another piece to the mosaic. And in fact, then students will encounter the phrase *(Rēx) eum in labyrinthum dūcī iussit* (XXV. 59). The remaining parts of the construction will come later, and so on.

Anyone can verify this principle by giving even a little child only the central pieces of a puzzle, albeit large and clearly defined ones. The child will have no difficulty in putting them together. If then the child is given the pieces belonging to one corner, he will have little difficulty in placing them correctly. Proceeding in this way even a child can put together a mosaic of great dimensions. But if one were to give the same child the thousands of pieces all at once, including those of minute dimensions, he would have great difficulty in assembling them, and would likely lose patience and interest.

In the teaching of physics the didactic principle of approximation is well known. Sometimes it is better and more didactically effective to omit some details in order to show the heart of a problem. Thus the mind is undistracted by qualifications, however true and accurate, that would cause one to lose sight of the most important facts. Once this nucleus has been understood, in turn, one can then proceed through gradual adjustments and so

fit out the skeleton with muscles, nerves, veins, and skin.

At what point in this process, then, should the teacher make use of the systematic treatment of syntax? Two solutions seem possible: (1) immediately after having found examples in the text and having led students to reflect on them so as to inductively understand the rule themselves; in this case one should take care to focus the attention of the students only on that part of the rule that they have already encountered; or (2) at the end, after having met examples of every kind, understood and practiced them. In most cases teachers may find it most efficient to present such discussion of grammar in English. The *Index Grammaticus* on pp. 326-327 of *FAMILIA ROMANA* provides a convenient repertoire of the syntactic themes covered in the book; it is supplemented by the catalogue of Latin syntax in Appendix VII of this volume which provides the Latin and English names for all constructions together with *exempla*.

SYNTAXIS LATINA

At this point we should like to emphasize two other aspects of the reference grammar (*SYNTAXIS LATINA*). First of all it should be underlined that it has not been developed to facilitate translation into Latin—like some Latin grammars—but rather for a better and more profound conscious understanding of the structure of the language that students encounter in their readings. We are somewhat diffident about the value of translation from Latin into English in the early stages of language learning, since the common procedure of translating to understand is likely to create bad habits. One should aim first for understanding, which may then make translation possible, as understood in its etymological sense of transporting the same concept, reformulated, into another language. We are even somewhat doubtful about the value of translation from English into Latin at the very earliest stages, since this risks becoming a mechanical application of rules by students who as yet have no sense of the language's character. That active competence that we regard as fundamental in the mastery of a language—as a means, not necessarily an end—consists above all in the unmediated production of the language, through conversation, composition, responses to questions, exercises of completion and manipulation. Such practice habituates students insofar as possible to think in Latin from the very first days, without forced expressions that only hide Latin in English or vice versa. For this reason our *SYNTAXIS LATINA* is primarily descriptive, and does not have recourse to parallels or contrasts with English usage, except where this seems of particular didactic value. For the same reason in most cases the examples are not translated, since the formal study of the rule should take place after the student is capable of understanding the formal contexts in which it appears.

Secondly, the reference grammar illustrates rules with phrases and examples drawn from the course itself. Only rarely has it seemed opportune to extend the range of examples to include some drawn from classical authors not represented in *FAMILIA ROMANA* and *ROMA AETERNA*. Care has been taken, especially for the syntax of the case system, to add as many contextual examples as possible to the explanations. It is up to the teacher to bring whatever examples seem most apposite to the students's attention. Beyond the examples drawn from the context of the course a series of syntactical examples is presented in Appendix IV to this manual. These simplified examples may serve as mnemonic aids for the memorization of rules. We consider it more effective to retain a simple and clear example in one's memory, from which the "rule" can be applied to all other examples, than to commit to memory an abstract definition removed from any concrete linguistic practice. It is always a painful spectacle to find that a student can perfectly repeat the "rule" of *videor* or of the passive periphrastic, even in the most complicated manner, and then be unable to furnish a correct example.

Vocabulary lists

The Latin vocabulary in the index to *FAMILIA ROMANA* (*Index vocabulōrum*) lists all the Latin words in the course in alphabetical order, indicating the initial context in which the word appears with a given meaning. This list makes it possible for students to find immediately the passage that explains a word which they may have momentarily forgotten. The instructor can at any time have recourse to this index in order to find the first appearance of a word or of a grammatical rule (pp. 326-327) that needs elaboration in class.

The Latin-English vocabulary list, available separately, is a kind of life-preserver that should only be used very exceptionally. The sense of new words can be understood directly from the context, and it is much more effective for the student to thus understand Latin through Latin. This list should only be used by students working on their own in order to verify an interpretation that they may be unsure of or when, in the absence of an instructor, they feel unable to understand the word on their own. As with any such extreme measure, we hope that students will never have need of it.

SPEAKING LATIN

The purpose of the *LINGUA LATINA* course is to develop the ability to read Latin with ease and understanding. Although it has been adopted by many proponents of the use of Latin as a spoken language, this is not its goal. Excellent teachers have taught the books effectively using very little spoken Latin in the classroom. Nevertheless, we believe that the more Latin is used in the classroom, the more effective instruction can be. Correct pronunciation on the part of the instructor is therefore essential, since students will generally have no other model for their own Latin ear and voice. Even teachers who are not comfortable speaking Latin extemporaneously should be able to read passages from the text correctly and expressively. As Prof. Ian Thomson puts it,

> Basically, this means modeling the Latin sentence by sentence (or paragraph by paragraph) for the students to echo in chorus or by individuals. The teacher's model must be accurate, expressive, and brisk without being too fast. If the response is timid or straggling, model the Latin again until a confident response is forthcoming.
>
> There will be choral repetition with and without the printed text, partial choral response, and individual reading. The teacher will use the overhead projector freely, particularly for the presentation of new material with visual aids... Variety is essential in the means of presentation, but the basic principle of model and response should remain constant.

Teachers should have no problem in giving standard classroom commands in Latin, but for the first several times they may wish to reinforce them with an 'English equivalent (e.g. *"Audīte,* listen!"). Ideally, nothing but Latin should eventually be heard in class, but this is not always possible.[12] It is always better to use English for instruction or comment than to fumble for appropriate Latin. The only thing that would contravene the method is persistent anglicizing of the Latin.

Thus, before beginning to teach the instructor must have a clear grasp of two fundamental aspects of the spoken language: pronunciation and stress accent.

The pronunciation of Latin

Pages 4-6 of the student's manual *LATINE DISCO* set forth rules for the pronunciation of Latin. Without wanting to enter the *vexāta quaestiō* of the "best" or "worst" pronunciation of Latin, it is a fact that, since the international conference at Avignon in 1956 most countries in Europe and North America have adopted the so-called restored pronunciation, which is believed to be a reasonable approximation of that in use in the first century B.C. In the Catholic Church and in countries such as Italy where its influence remains strong the so-called ecclesiastical or Late Latin pronunciation remains in use; it too is described at the beginning of *LATINE DISCO*. This pronunciation has its own value and a historical tradition going back to late antiquity, handed down through the Gregorian liturgy and the transmission *vīvae vōcis ōrāculō* of *scholae* and monasteries since the Middle Ages. This tradition is not likely to disappear, and in fact its application is particularly defensible if, as Professor Tunberg suggests in Appendix V, one intends to read not only ancient authors but also works of the middle ages, Renaissance, and the modern neo-Latin tradition. Thus, whichever pronunciation the instructor decides to use, it is advisable that students be given some understanding of the value and historical place of both of them. Even those students using the Late Latin pronunciation should, at least by the time they encounter passages of classical poetry in chapter 34 of *FAMILIA ROMANA*, have some understanding of the scholarship behind the restored pronunciation, and how it can help us appreciate the quantitative meters of Latin poetry.

The law of the penultimate syllable— importance of correct stress accent (ictus)

Whatever pronunciation students are using it is important that they learn vowel quantities, which are often essential to understanding Latin forms (e.g., cf. *malum* and *mālum* juxtaposed in chapters 6 and 7 respectively) and always essential to placement of the correct stress accent on Latin words in accordance with the law of the penultimate syllable. Normally this rule is formulated as follows: Latin accent is always on the penultimate (second-to-last) syllable if it is long; if it is short, the accent is placed on the previous, antepenultimate syllable. This apparently simple definition, often repeated in grammars and textbooks, can sometimes create pedagogical difficulties. It does not, for example, distinguish between syllable length and vowel length. Students should understand that a syllable may be long not only if the vowel is long by nature, but also if it is long by position, i.e. followed by

---

12   Teachers will find the Latin names for standard grammatical terminology together with exempla in Appendix VII.

two consonants which are not mute and liquid. Pious reticence is perhaps called for here at the outset. Such complications are avoided by Ørberg's elegant formulation on p. 6 of *LATINE DISCO*: "The penultimate is accented unless it ends in a *short vowel*, in which case the *antepenultimate* is accented." Throughout the course all vowels that are long by nature are marked with a macron (horizontal bar above the letter). It will suffice at the beginning to make sure that students understand the rules of syllabic division, neatly illustrated in the third *lectiō* of chapter one, in order to recognize a penultimate syllable ending in a consonant, a long vowel, or diphthong (in which case it receives a stress accent) or in a short vowel (in which case the antepenultimate syllable is accented.)

However one chooses to present this law it is worth keeping in mind that, at this initial stage, the most important thing is to bring the student to the study of Latin without shock, drawing the greatest possible pleasure and satisfaction from it. Time will not be lacking at a later stage to elaborate the rules of accentuation with greater precision, which may here be presented with some approximation. The use of the word "approximation" should not be taken to indicate that the course aims for some vague understanding rather than an exact and rigorous knowledge of morphology, syntax, vocabulary and phraseology. On the contrary, it is simply an issue of didactic efficiency, the choice of the time and manner of learning. The goals of the course are indeed ambitious but, experience has shown, achievable: that students correctly understand Latin prose texts in the briefest possible time, through the practice of writing as well as reading and, to some degree, of listening to and speaking Latin.

BEGINNING USE OF THE COURSE

The teacher may choose to begin class with a brief introduction to Latin pronunciation, or immediately begin reading the first chapter of *FAMILIA ROMANA*, in which case points of pronunciation will have to be emphasized as they arise. The lesson begins by inviting students to open their book and look over the map on page 6 so that they can immediately find the geographical names to be used in the first chapter; ideally an overhead transparency of this map may be projected. The students may spend some time familiarizing themselves with the map. The instructor should then read aloud: *Rōma in Italiā est.* It is important to pronounce these words clearly and distinctly, with correct stress accent. The students may then be encouraged to repeat the instructor's words all together; choral reading encourages participation and diminishes self-consciousness. Individual students should not be called on to read aloud until they have developed the confidence to do so without embarrassment.

Students should have little difficulty understanding this first sentence. One might point out that *est* is at the end of the sentence, and clarify that in Latin the position of the verb is much freer than in English. One could also say *Rōma est in Italiā.* The instructor continues with two equally simply sentences: *Italia in Eurōpa est. Graecia in Eurōpa est.* And then the same thing is said in a single sentence: *Italia et Graecia in Eurōpa sunt.* Students will immediately understand the meaning of *et*, and should be able to guess why *sunt* has now taken the place of *est*. All the same it is worth lingering over this last point, to make sure that every last student has no doubt whatsover of the meaning of this sentence.

Linguam Latīnam docēre lentum opus

The teacher should proceed with care. These first expressions are indeed so similar to the vernacular that students can understand them almost passively, so to speak. But it is precisely here in these first sentences that it is necessary to habituate the students to reflect on the text and to understand the Latin in Latin, not merely by ear but on reflection, not by instinct but by reasoning. For this reason it is essential to always draw their attention to the marginal notes, where the grammatical concepts being learned in the accompanying context are placed in relief. Already in these first pages they should habituate themselves to the process of contextual induction. Otherwise they will continue superficially, deceived by the ease of this initial phase, taking little trouble. After a few pages, however, they will no longer know how to proceed. For this reason the braking intervention of the instructor is crucial at this early stage. The student does not understand and cannot understand how important it is at this early stage to reflect and be aware of the phenomena he is encountering; he understands, and thinks this is enough. The teacher must make him understand that, as the course progresses, this understanding based on similarity and analogy with English will not be sufficient, if not accompanied by a conscious learning of the mechanisms that govern the language. Without frightening the students, one should underline the importance of thinking about every sentence and every marginal note. One should stimulate the students's satisfaction at being able to understand without help each "rule" through the context in which it is presented. Each time they can do this will be a small personal success, which will reinforce their desire to learn Latin.

Understanding Latin through Latin

Don't imagine that one can save time and energy by avoiding an effort that seems superfluous. For example, when students look over the map on page 6 at the beginning of the lesson, be sure that they don't merely pick out *Rōma* and *Italia* and neglect the rest. They should attentively look at all the geographical names so they will recognize them in the context of their reading. They should be in a position to understand Latin through Latin, and since they do not yet know a single word of Latin one should make sure that they understand every word as they read it, following the instructions scrupulously and with vigilant intelligence.

One then continues by reading the sentences in the successive lines on page 7: *Hispānia quoque in Eurōpa est. Hispānia et Italia et Graecia in Eurōpa sunt. Aegyptus in Eurōpā non est, Aegyptus in Āfricā est. Gallia nōn in Āfricā est. Gallia est in Eurōpā. Syria nōn est in Eurōpā, sed in Asiā.* The instructor should always read these sentences first out loud; only then may the students be invited to repeat in choral fashion. Two difficulties present themselves in these first passages: the students may not immediately understand the meaning of *quoque* and *sed*. But they can be brought to understand these words on their own if they concentrate on the text, reading these sentences in relation to the previous ones and keeping an eye on the map. One can invite them to pay attention, without translating: *Italia in Eurōpa est. Graecia in Eurōpa est.Hispānia quoque in Eurōpa est.* In short, it is indispensable that they understand Latin as Latin.

Let's suppose that the meaning of *quoque* is still not clear, that some students think they understand it but are not sure. Not to worry. The text is constructed in such a way that the same word will recurr several times in opportunely varied expressions, so as to explain itself. One has just read: *Syria nōn est in Eurōpa, sed in Asiā*. One invites students to look for *Syria* on the map. Immediately afterwards the text reads: *Arabia quoque in Asiā est*. One looks at the map again, and thinks about the text. By now the meaning of *quoque* should be clear. The students can be asked about this point. By now one can also point out that *quoque* always follows the word to which it refers.

Lines 10 and 11 include the sentences: *Est-ne Graecia in Eurōpa?* and *Est-ne Rōma in Graeciā?* The students will understand that these sentences are questions, because they end with question marks, but they should also observe that Latin has a special particle that follows the first word of a particular kind of question: *-ne*. At the beginning, in the most elementary texts, every question is followed by a corresponding response. Often the sense of the question will only become clear with certainty on reading the answer. For example, the question in line 12, *Ubi est Rōma?* can be understood with certainty only on the basis of the response: *Rōma in Italiā est*. Students may be asked to contrast questions introduced by *–ne* with interrogatives like *ubi?* On reflection it will be apparent to them that the particle *–ne* introduces questions expecting a yes or no response, where questions introduced by *ubi?* cannot be answered in this way.

The marginal explanations

Students can face the text right away and surpass the difficulties as they present themselves. It suffices that they read and think about what they read. If they find themselves in doubt about the meaning of individual words or phrases, they should be invited to look first of all for a marginal note or illustration that resolves their difficulty. One cannot sufficiently emphasize the importance of these marginal notes to the structure of the course. Every obstacle that the student may encounter has been foreseen by the author, who provides the means for overcoming it through marginal explanations or appropriate pictures. For example, at the very beginning of chapter one there is an illustration that clarifies the meaning of the words *fluvius, īnsula,* and *oppidum*. If none of these means permit the student to resolve the problem, it is only necessary to continue until one finds the word again—encountering the word again in a new context, they will understand it without difficulty.

It may be noticed, not without wonder, that in this introduction to the study of the first page of the Latin text we have not translated a single word. One can in fact understand a language perfectly well without translating it. One does not waste time or energy by asking "how does one say in English." From the very beginning the student should be habituated to associate the Latin words directly with the things they signify. Which is to say they should understand Latin through Latin, *per sē*—they should become accustomed to thinking in Latin. In this way it will be seen that the new language will be learned with surprising speed and security.

We do not translate in order to understand, but rather understand so as to translate

Naturally every undertaking should be made with some mental agility; we are not claiming that the teacher should consider it prohibited to occasionally give the meaning of Latin words in English. It should not be overlooked, however, that translation is understood in this course as a final verification, through which the student who has already perfectly understood the Latin text, without the need to translate it into English, attempts to reformulate the same ideas and concepts in his native language. In short, as we have repeatedly said, the student does not translate in order to understand, but rather understands the text in the original Latin so as to then translate it, if so asked. We don't believe there is any other serious approach to translation, and we deny that what students are accustomed to do in our schools amounts to real translation.

Therefore, it is of capital importance to avoid using translation as a normal instrument. The student should not be habituated to the necessity of transferring words and phrases into his own language in order to understand them. Our goal is that, after two years of daily study, students be ready to read Livy, Nepos, Sallust and even Cicero with alacrity and simplicity, with no more or less difficulty than they would encounter in reading Shakespeare. It is not that they grope laboriously in the attempt to decipher, with a dictionary in hand, ten lines taken out of context, and often devoid of interest. We want students to take pleasure in intense reading, that they be capable of reading page after page and entire works without excessive difficulty. But this goal will never be reached if from the first days students feel the need to "translate" in order to understand. They should understand directly in Latin. Later, if the necessity arises—for example, in communicating with people ignorant of Latin—they can then have recourse to translation.

Disadvantages of the grammar/translation method

Sidney Morris made an in-depth study of the teaching of Latin,[13] and found the following disadvantages in the traditional grammar/translation method:

1. Latin is treated not as a means for communicating ideas, but as an ensemble of exercises illustrating grammar and syntax.

2. The amount of time spent in the analysis and translation of Latin precludes doing much serious reading of Latin texts.

3. Students become incapable of understanding Latin without translating it, unless they are helped by the instructor or a battery of notes.

4. Almost the whole of the work of translation has little relevance for the students: the analytic nature of the method is tedious for most students.

We would like to direct our attention above all to the third point. The *forma mentis* of translation as a *sine quā nōn* for comprehension often cannot be eliminated even after years of reading Latin. Teachers may verify this observation in their own practice, and ask themselves why they are always prone to translate Latin sentences into English in order to understand a text. The answer is simple: because in the depths of our consciousness Latin words do not correspond to things and concepts, but to other, English words. We are thus inclined to filter Latin through our mother tongue. The goal of the *LINGVA LATINA PER SE ILLVSTRATA* course is to reduce this filtration to a minimum, and to bring the students to the Latin text without any kind of

13   Morris, S. 1966. *Viae Novae: New Techniques in Latin Teaching*, Hulton Educational Publications, London, 1966, p. 9.

diaphragm. We may not always succeed, but this should be the ideal at which we aim.

Can a text really be per sē explicātus?

But is it really possible that a text can be comprehensible through itself, as if it were self-explanatory? Here are the words of Ian Thomson of Indiana University, who used the course over many years; note that his quotation from the text is based on an earlier edition of *FAMILIA ROMANA*:

But is Ørberg's text really self-explanatory? Can translation really be eliminated? The best answer is to examine it. At random, I have chosen Vol. II, *capitulum* XXX, 1-12:

Ex agrīs *reversus* Iūlius continuō *balneum* petit, id est locus, ubi corpus lavātur. Dominus prīmum aquā *tepidā*, tum *calidā* , dēnique frigidā lavātur...

Dum Iūlius vestem novam induit, Cornēlius et Orontēs, amīcī et *hospitēs* eius, cum uxōribus Fabiā et Paulā ad villam veniunt. Hospitēs sunt amīcī, quōrum alter alterum semper bene *recipit* in domum suam. Numquam hospēs hospitī īanuam claudit, etiam sī *inexpectātus* venit.

Hodiē autem hospitēs Iūliī exspectātī veniunt, nam Iūlius eōs invitāvit ad *cēnam*. Cēna est cibus, quem Rōmānī circiter hōrā decimā sūmunt).

I have italicized all the new words introduced in this passage. The narrative, entitled *Convivium* (itself a new word), is introduced by a picture of two slaves decorating a dining room. No object is depicted which the students cannot already identify with a Latin word, or will not be able to, once they have read the narrative. The visual aid is severely functional, as are the marginal entries which appear opposite the new words. From the very beginning of the course students must be taught to rely on the visual aids and the marginalia.

Let us imagine that these twelve lines are part of the students's assignment for preparation at home. He will first look at the picture, partly out of curiosity, partly because he has been taught to use every one of the aids provided, and partly because he knows from experience that it is certain to help him in some way. At first he will not be able to verbalize the concept beyond, perhaps, a simple phrase like *Ecce duo servī*, but this will not trouble him. The mental vignette is established, and the desire, subconscious and conscious, is created to flesh it out with words. He then begins to read rapidly, aloud, in the Latin order, and in sizeable chunks (I recommend a paragraph at a time, but each student has his own preferences and should be allowed to indulge them). After a few readings it is obvious which words and phrases convey no picture of what is happening. This is the point at which he studies the marginalia. The form *reversus* may give trouble, although *revertitur* has been introduced as early as *capit.* xxi.1, and he has seen forms analogous to *reversus* many times before. The marginal gloss is *revertī, revertisse vel reversum esse*, which is Nature Method shorthand—with which the teacher has made sure he is familiar—conveying the information that *revertī* is present infinitive and *revertisse* or *reversum esse* is perfect infinitive. The meaning of *reversus* alone should now become clear. If not, he will underline it in

pencil and move on. The word *balneum* is defined in the text. The next gloss, *tepidus = nec frigidus nec calidus* contains enough information to make the meaning of all three words plain. The word *hospitēs* is defined in the text. In the margin appears *ūnus hospes* and under it *duo hospitēs* which tells the student that *hospes* is masculine. Very probably it will be recognized as a noun declined like *comes*. Opposite *recipit* appears *recipere = accipere, admittere,* which makes the meaning of *recipit* clear, since *accipere* and *admittere* are already known. Since *exspectātus* has occurred before, *inexpectātus* should present no problem, but the gloss *inexpectātus = nōn exspectātus* leaves nothing to chance. Finally, *cēna* is defined in the text. Note that nine new words are introduced in 84 lines of text. Some occur more than once, and not always in the same case. The juxtapositions *alter alterum* and *hospes hospitī* make neat Latin and point to the importance of case endings.[14]

Thomson suggests that the process described above takes about ten minutes of classroom time, at most fifteen. This random example shows how it is possible to understand the texts in the Ørberg course without recourse to translation.

The difficulty of grammar

Latin grammar has the reputation of being very difficult. And it certainly is, for someone who has had to mechanically memorize its rich morphology and attempted to compose or even merely recognize the correct forms in separate, abstract sentences, devised for the sole purpose of scholastic exercise. Could a more unnatural method exist? Grammar should be learned through its application, in the living use of the language, in context, in such a way that the function of its different forms becomes clear from the texture of the sentence, in such a way that the forms are learned through their function, instead of through static, theoretical rules. It is one thing to study a mechanism in motion, another to see it at rest, in the illustration of a mechanical treatise.

In short, grammatical rules should be learned only at a second stage, when the practical functioning of the linguistic instrument is well understood, and can serve to rationalize under a common denominator certain notions that have already been learned in practice. If study proceeds in this practical and gradual way, Latin can be learned with a facility and ease comparable to that with which we learned English as children.

The grammatical section

In conformity with this principle, every chapter in *FAMILIA ROMANA* is followed by a grammatical section, entitled *Grammatica Latina* (not to be confused with the separate handbook of morphology by the same name). Here the new forms of expression learned in the text are reviewed and illustrated with further examples systematically arranged. It should be read immediately after completing the two or three *lectiōnēs* of the chapter. Prof. Thomson comments on this presentation of *Grammatica Latina*:

Since its text is also self-explanatory, it can be read through in Latin. Some teachers, however, may prefer to use

---

14   Thomson, Ian. 1976. *Further Thoughts on the Nature Method*. Classical World 70: 9-15.

English to explain the Latin grammar, with some reference to parallel or different usages in the English language.

After all the examples have been studied, the teacher may wish to elicit a formulation of the general rule. This will require careful guidance. The initial formulation should always come from the students, but the teacher may suggest the final wording.

At various points in the textbook whole declensions and tense systems are summarized. By then students should be able to recognize and understand any of the forms in context, but some teachers may feel more comfortable if the students can recite declensions and conjugations systematically. Recitation out of context is permissible at this stage, but since students are used to dealing with forms in context, the teacher may supply a subject at least for each verb form and a cue word to indicate what tense is required (e.g. *hodiē, crās, herī*), and a suitable short context into which the required noun, pronoun, or adjectival forms can be supplied.

The Pēnsa *and* Exercitia

The exercises in *EXERCITIA LATINA* should be completed after having read the corresponding *lectiō* several times; by then the material should be so well assimilated that it will not be necessary to consult the text in completing them. The review exercises in *FAMILIA ROMANA* (*Pēnsum A, B, C),* however, should be done only after the student has read the whole corresponding chapter repeatedly and with close attention. These exercises, by contrast with the commented reading of the text—which should always be done in class, out loud and with the help of the teacher—can be done as homework and in any case, with rare exception, without the help of the teacher. Care should be taken, however, that they always be corrected in class.

Pensum A and the first of the *exercitia* for each *lectiō* drill endings and morphology. Before attempting them students should again study the marginal notes (sometimes amplified by explanations given by the instructor in class) or, if they have completed the chapter, they should also review the *Grammatica Latina,* since these exercises are geared to practicing grammatical forms. It is advantageous for the student to recopy the question, filling in the correct endings and words where they are missing. In no circumstances should the student write directly in the book, since doing so will make it impossible to review usefully and repeat the same exercises. Recopying is at any rate more effective, since *quī scrībit bis legit,* but it may sometimes be tiresome for students. It is most important that students be able to supply the correct answer immediately on reading the sentence or question; thus it may be desirable sometimes for them only to write out a portion of the exercises, as long as they are prepared to answer all of them spontaneously.

Pēnsum B and the second set of *exercitia* for each *lectiō* are not concerned with terminations but with vocabulary. Students will find all the words necessary for completing them in the adjacent margin. These lists provide a comprehensive review of new vocabulary in each *capitulum* or *lectiō*. *Pēnsum* C and corresponding *exercitia* call on students to respond to questions with a complete sentence, in Latin.

Students should be capable of completing these exercises without looking for the correct answer in the text, which implies that they must have studied the text in depth. We repeat that all

the exercises of each chapter must be corrected in class, if possible individually, otherwise collectively. The student's written work should be closely examined, with necessary corrections and observations annotated. Home-school parents may make use of the answer keys available from Focus Publishing in correcting these exercises, although if they are working through the course with their children they may not have need for them. The *Pēnsa* are also available on separate sheets from Focus Publishing. This format may be convenient for assigning homework or for homeschool students; it may also be used in testing.

We should underline that the exercises are an essential instrument for verifying the linguistic competence of the students and to assure them a more solid mastery of Latin. For this reason it is important that they always do these exercises with the greatest possible care. They should be asked to do them on their own, and not with the help of a classmate or a private tutor, since it is essential that they train themselves to master the vocabulary and structures encountered.

Forgotten words

If in reading the course one happens on a word that students have previously encountered but no longer remember, it is not necessary to look for it in earlier chapters. It is enough to consult the *Index vocabulōrum* at the back of the text; there the word will be found with a Roman numeral indicating the chapter and an arabic numeral indicating the line number where the word appeared for the first time. If more than one chapter is listed, that is an indication that the word has appeared with more than one meaning. In any case, it will suffice to reread the original appearance of the word, perhaps with some of the surrounding context, in order for students to refresh their memory and recall its sense.

But how can one be sure that students have correctly understood a Latin word? This is the general problem of verifying comprehension of the text. One can proceed by several paths. First of all, the questions in Pēnsum C and those of the exercitia are in fact questions on comprehension, to which it is difficult to respond if one has not well understood the text to which it refers. But the teacher cannot be content with a general understanding: he must be certain that students has fully understood what they have read, and have a clear understanding of each word, without misunderstandings or mistakes.

For the purpose of verification one can pose additional questions, in the course of the reading, on specific points. The questions will preferably be formulated in Latin, but may be in English. For example, in the first chapter, to determine that the sense of *ubi,* or *quid,* or *num* has been well understood, one can extemporaneously raise questions such as *"Ubi est Tiberis?" "Ubi sunt Rōma et Tūsculum?" "Num Sparta in Italiā est?" "Num Melita īnsula māgna est?" "Ubi est Germānia?" "Quid est Brundisium?" "Quid est Rhodus?" "Num Sardinia īnsula parva est?"* and so forth. In chapter XXXII, to give a somewhat more complex example, to verify that students have really understood the meaning of *timēre nē* (which the teacher may already have clarified with various examples on the blackboard or overhead projector) one might ask the students, *"Cūr timet Mēdus? Quid mīlitēs factūrōs esse crēdit, sī eum cēperint?"* It is not necessary that the student respond by using the construction *timēre nē*: if the student were to respond, for example, *"Ille mīlitēs sē Rōmam abductūrōs esse putat, ut ad mortem in amphiteātrō cōram populō mittātur, sīcut Iūlius servīs suīs minārī solēbat"*, such a response would imply that the student had correctly understood the sentence in the text *"Timeō nē mīlitēs mē captum Rōmam abdūcant"* (XXXII. 212-213).

At this stage extemporaneous translation may be used as a means of verification. This is done at a final stage not as a tool for comprehension of the text, but only for the purpose of verification, on the part of the instructor, of how much of the text the student has really understood. Before asking students to translate one should always ask whether they have understood what they have read. If they respond negatively, they should be asked to read the sentence again, new questions should be posed, synonyms should be used to clarify obscure words, attention should be drawn to the marginal notes. Only when students are sure of having understood should they be asked to translate, formulating the question along these lines: "how would you say the same thing in English? How can this concept be rendered?" etc.

But how can students be sure that they have understood? It is simple—if that which they have read has a complete meaning, in itself and in relation to that which precedes and follows, then they have exactly understood every word. For the Ørberg text is conceived so that it will only have a complete and rational sense when every word is given its proper meaning. This exercise of contextual logical coherence not only refines the students' capacity for understanding, thus developing their intelligences; it also avoids the possibility of merely mechanical translation, which unfortunately is the standard operating procedure of students habituated to received methods and often yields monstrous "translations" void of sense.

At any time the teacher may doubt the students' ability to understand exactly what they are reading and so desire to verify the accuracy of their answers. He may then, as we have said, have recourse to translation. But, let us repeat, this is merely a means of verification, not an incentive to mental laziness or, even worse, to the habit of mentally transferring words into one's own language in order to understand them. The student must first have found a solution before the teacher can verify it. And we insist on the fact that a student of normal abilities should be able to do this.

In order to present the marginal explanations in a clear and concise manner, the text makes use of four conventional signs. An equals sign (=) between two words or expressions indicates that they have a more or less identical sense. In English one might say "mom = mother." The sign (:) means viz. or "that is to say," and serves to better explain a word or to give the meaning of a word in a particular context. An English example would be "good : not bad." The sign (↔) indicates that the two words or expressions have an opposite meaning; in English we might say "good ↔ bad." Finally, one encounters from time to time the sign (<), which means "derived from" and shows that a word derives from another which is already known; as we might write in English: "goodness < good." All these signs should be explained as they are encountered.

Besides all these aids that sudents find in the chapters of the course, there is the student's manual *LATINE DISCO*, a series of instructions that bring their attention to noteworthy points. Much of the material in this student's manual was originally intended to be part of a teacher's guide. Now it can be used by both teachers and students. The former can use it to plan their lessons and present students with grammatical clarifications; the latter will find it helpful in reviewing and fixing the teacher's explanations in the memory.

Everything in the class has been calculated so that student can learn Latin quickly and well, with the greatest return for the least effort. This does not mean, however, that it does not demand effort, and that students will not experience difficulties. After all, the structure of Latin is so different from that of modern languages that it demands, especially at the outset, a certain force of perseverance. But this is only a first difficulty. One must always exhort students not to be afraid, never to give up. Such confidence can be communicated to students only if the teacher himself possesses it. If the students persevere and follow the direction of their teacher and the instructions in the book to the letter, one can guarantee them that they will succeed in overcoming every difficulty in the space of a few weeks, and that they will familiarize themselves perfectly with the structure of the Latin language— with a new way of thinking, of expressing themselves, of seeing everyday reality and intellectual life. This is what it means to acquire a new mental dimension, a new linguistic personality.

PLANNING A TYPICAL LESSON

It is essential that the teacher begin each lesson with a clear idea of what is to be accomplished. Prof. Ian Thomson has some useful remarks on this subject:

Lesson plans should all be different to some degree, but most will follow this pattern: (a) Some review of previous work (for example, oral or written practice of work set for home study, or of work done in the previous lesson). (b) The introduction of new work. (This may be done in stages: new work, drill or exercises, more new work, etc.) (c) Drill or exercises to consolidate the new work. (If these are not well done, the teacher may reteach the point they are designed to consolidate, then return to the drill or exercises, either in the same lesson or in the next. Some teachers find that students perform better, if practice on work which has not been well done is put off to the next day.) (d) Some preparation of the work to be set for home study. (This is particularly important for high school students, who should not be expected to deal with new material outside of class. The homework should consolidate what has been done in class, and the students should have a reasonable chance of doing it well. This may mean an oral discussion in class of work which will be written at home, or practice in reading material which will be copied or adapted out of class, or a discussion of material which the students will have to read by themselves.) The homework assignment should be clearly stated and given out well before the final bell...

No class meeting should be entirely devoted to reading the text. The readings should last about ten minutes each and be interspersed with manipulation exercises, written or oral, perhaps a sentence or two of dictation, a word game, a short discussion of some point in the text, or some other activity which consolidates the new points in the text. Care must be taken, however, that the lessons do not become too fragmented and heterogeneous. When the narrative sections are being presented, the main business of the class should be reading.

Here is a sample lesson plan for working with a chapter of *LINGVA LATINA PER SE ILLVSTRATA*, in this example for chapter 9. An alternate style of lesson plan from Prof. Thomson can be found in the Appendix I.

1. Invite the students to look attentively at the image given at the beginning of the chapter. Or, if possible, project that image on a screen with the help of an overhead projector so the whole class can focus its attention on it. By focusing the students's attention on a single image an overhead projector can make it easier to question students rapidly.[15] Normally students will already know some words relevant to the image; others will be suggested to them as the lesson continues. The instructor and students may comment, in Latin, on the scene represented, introducing the subject to be treated in the lesson. The instructor or the students themselves may pose questions, in Latin, on what they see. For example, while looking at the image at the beginning of chapter IX, one might ask: *Quō it pāstor? Quid portat? Habetne pāstor baculum? Ubi est silva? Ubi est sōl?* The predictable responses will be: *Pāstor ad umbram it. Pāstor saccum umerīs portat et baculum habet. Silva est post rīvum. Sōl est in caelō.* Students are asked to take account of new words and to try to memorize them.

2. The instructor reads <u>aloud,</u> attentively and expressively, a passage of the chapter. At early stages while students are still learning Latin pronunciation they may repeat aloud together in choral fashion what the instructor reads to them; once students are comfortable with pronunciation one may ask an individual student to read the passage aloud with correct intonation. This procedure should be varied, so that it doesn't become annoying and demotivating. The instructor should be capable of reading in an engaging manner, not too quickly—lest the students be unable to follow—nor too slowly—lest the reading become tedious and soporific. To gather the sense of a literature composed for the ear, and not the letter, as was Latin literature, it is necessary to read well.[16]

3. The instructor should verify that all have understood every word and phrase of the reading with the help of the marginal notes and the context. One can pose questions in Latin or in English: *Quis est vir quī in campō ambulat? Estne sōlus in campō? Quot ovēs habet pāstor? Num omnēs ovēs albae sunt? Quid dat pāstor ovibus suīs?* The answers to these questions will already make it clear whether students have correctly understood the text.

4. The students' attention is drawn to the marginal notes. From the first day they should be trained to note and take them into account in the course of reading. In the example that we are considering, the concept of declension is being introduced and the attention of the students is concentrated on parisyllabic nouns of the third declension. One must insist on the importance of mastering the case system and make the comparison between the cases of the first two declensions and those of *ovis*. Using the adjective *albus-a-um* one can ask the students to make it agree with the cases of *ovis*. One should avoid using a preconceived order, however. Students should be capable of saying, and *ā fortōrī*, of recognizing the cases outside of any schematism. Ask: *ovibus...?* Answer: *...albīs.* Ask: *ovium...?* Response: *...albārum.* Ask: *ovem...?* Response: *...albam,* and so on. This kind of exercise has two functions: to familiarize students with the new forms and to verify and practice that which they have already learned.

5. If it is clear that students have understood the text directly in Latin one can proceed directly to step 6; if not, one should return to expressive reading, giving variations and explanations in Latin. Although no student of normal intelligence could fail to understand the very easy passages at the beginning of chapter IX if presented as above suggested, let's take for an example lines 1-7 of *Pāstor et ovēs.* The teacher could explain in the following way: *Iūlius habet pāstōrem: ecce pāstor. Iūlius est dominus huius pāstoris. Pāstor est in campō. Cum eō sunt canis et ovēs.* And so forth.

6. At this point one might also, if desirable, ask students to translate—though one should avoid always doing so. "If someone who doesn't know Latin should ask you what is written in these lines, and wanted to know word by word, how would you render this passage?"

7. Proceed passage by passage and explain individually the new morphosyntactic forms or new words as they are encountered. Here it is useful to use the blackboard or to mark a transparency on the overhead projector.

8. Complete the reading and analysis of a *lēctiō* (as indicated by a Roman numeral in the margin; e.g. the first *lēctiō* in chapter 9 goes from line 1 to line 38.) One useful way of completing a *lēctiō* is to give students five to ten minutes to read and reread the entire passage silently to themselves

---

15 A set of overhead transparencies including the main illustrations from each chapter is available from Focus Publishing.

16 Students may be interested to learn that this was the ancient practice of reading, as described by Jean Leclercq, O.S.B., *The Love of Learning and the Desire for God*, Fordham University Press, New York, 1982, p. 15: "With regard to literature, a fundamental observation must be made...: in the Middle Ages, as in antiquity, they read usually, not as today, principally with the eyes, but with the lips, pronouncing what they saw, and with the ears, listening to the words pronounced, hearing what is called the "voices of the pages" (*vōcēs pāginārum*). It is a real acoustical reading; *legere* means at the same time *audire*. One understands only

what one hears, as we still say in French: "*entendre le latin,*" which means to "comprehend" it. No doubt, silent reading, or reading in a low voice, was not unknown; in that case it is designated by expressions like those of St. Benedict: *tacitē legere* or *legere sibi*, and according to St. Augustine: *legere in silentiō*, as opposed to the *clāra lēctiō*. But most frequently, when *legere* and *lēctiō* are used without further explanation, they mean an activity which, like chant and writing, requires the participation of the whole body and the whole mind. Doctors of ancient times used to recommend reading to their patients as a physical exercise on an equal level with walking, running, or ball-playing..."

with the goal of committing its contents to memory. Once they have read through the passage at least three times they are asked to close their books, and the instructor interrogates them rapidly on the content of the *lēctiō*. If the instructor has not yet learned the passage thoroughly he may at this point keep the book open while posing students questions about the passage; a projected image of the illustration pertaining to the *lēctiō* may help the students refresh their memory. It is desirable that through such a procedure students may virtually commit the passage to memory.

9. The exercises in *EXERCITIA LATINA* corresponding to this *lēctiō* should be assigned. One should be certain that students complete all of these exercises individually at home. In the following class one can go over them together.

10. The same procedure should be followed in each subsequent *lēctiō*. Once one has reached the final *lēctiō* of the chapter, the section *Grammatica Latina* should be read and the examples there presented in systematic order should be compared with those already encountered in the reading. Here grammatical concepts may be elaborated in English, though teachers may find it useful to convey the Latin names of constructions, found in the *Index grammaticus* to *FAMILIA ROMANA* and in Appendix VII of this volume.

11. Students are invited to reread at home the entire chapter, both the text and the *Grammatica* section. They should pay particular attention to the content, avoiding any misunderstanding. They should heed above all the new words and forms encountered in the marginal notes and grammatical explanations that have been explained by the teacher in class.

12. Students can review the material the instructor has presented in class in the instructions presented in the student's manual *LATINE DISCO*. They should study these pages with attention and memorize its contents.

13. Students should complete *Pēnsum A,* which recapitulates the material presented in the section *Grammatica Latina*. Once students have done this exercise individually these exercises should be gone over with the class as a whole. Students may then be invited to review the new vocabulary for the chapter, listed in the margin next to *Pēnsum B*. A useful exercise for the students to review this vocabulary with the instructor is by constructing a simple phrase using each word. They should then fill in the missing words in *Pēnsum B* so as to give a clear meaning. The final exercise is to respond to the questions of *Pēnsum C* with brief Latin sentences, whether orally or in writing.

14. While going over new material one should not neglect to ask students to give an oral resume, in Latin, of what they have read in preceding chapters. Then one may ask them questions about comprehension of the text. Such oral practice permits perfect assimilation so as to convert the structures and rules of the language into automatic mechanisms. As vocabulary and grammatical knowledge develop students will become capable of speaking with ever more accuracy and facility, so that a real and true dialogue can develop between instructor and students.

15. To consolidate what has been learned in the chapter (*capitulum*) students can read the corresponding *colloquium*

in the booklet *Colloquia Latīna*. These twenty-four dialogues make it possible to review grammar and vocabulary through pleasant and amusing dialogues. It is often rewarding for students to perform and even memorize these dialogues. Another exercise, once students have been introduced to the accusative/infinitive construction in Chapter XI, is to go back over earlier *Colloquia* inviting students to transform the dialogue into *ōrātiō obliqua* (indirect discourse). One may also ask students to give an oral or written summary of each dialogue. A booklet listing the Latin-English vocabulary from the *Colloquia* is available from Focus Publishing, but may not be necessary.

16. When it seems appropriate the instructor may choose to develop aspects of Roman civilization and culture that the course alludes to. Attention to costumes, historical and archaeological aspects is of course fundamental. Study of Roman civilization should be helpful to the understanding of the texts, in the sense that one cannot deeply understand a text without understanding the material aspects of the world that produced it. A list of books which may be useful to explain particular points of Latin civilization can be fund in appendix IV

SUPPLEMENTAL EXERCISES

As indispensable as the volumes *EXERCITIA LATINA* seems to us, it should be recognized that *LINGUA LATINA PER SE ILLUSTRATA* was used effectively by homeschoolers and in schools and universities for many years before these volumes appeared. Teachers used their own ingenuity to devise effective drills and exercises, and indeed the course by its nature lends itself to the creativity of both student and instructor. Many different kinds of exercises may be used to supplement the *EXERCITIA LATINA* and *PENSA,* according to the strengths and didactic personality of the instructor. We present here some exercises that we have found particularly useful and enjoyable.

- *Exercitia complētīva:* the teacher may compose supplementary exercises comparable to those in the volumes *EXERCITIA LATINA*. Volumes of supplementary exercises have been composed by a Belgian team of teachers; they are available in Italian from www.vivariumnovum.it under the title *Quaderni di esercizi per LINGUA LATINA PER SE ILLUSTRATA,* and may become available in English.

- *Dictātiō:* students may be asked to write out, with orthographical precision, a text read aloud. At the beginning stages this should be a passage that they have already encountered in *FAMILIA ROMANA,* though the teacher may freely choose a text from a chapter not yet covered or from some other source once students have a basic mastery of the Latin sound system.

- *Narrātiō:* students may be asked to narrate, out loud or in writing, the events told in each chapter in their own words. This can be a useful review when students are completing a chapter.

- *Interpretātiō in sermōnem patrium:* students may be asked to translate a given passage into English. This should be done only occasionally and as a means of confirming the students's understanding, though at an advanced stage it may be done as an exercise in the art of translation, studying the different possibilities for rendering Latin expressions.

- **Retroversio:** students may be asked to translate back into Latin a passage that they have already studied. The teacher reads out loud or presents in written form an accurate English translation of a passage that students have already studied. Students are then asked to translate it back into Latin.

The following exercises require an active mastery of Latin on the part of the instructor. Care should be taken that students not be set to translate into Latin passages for which they do not yet have the linguistic competence.

- **Interpretātiō in Latīnum:** students may be asked to translate an English passage, of difficulty corresponding to their current level, into Latin.

- **Summārium scrībere:** students may be asked to summarize or paraphrase, in Latin, a text already studied, a text read aloud in class, or the contents of a projected image. This can be done in writing or orally.

- **Compositiō sententiārum vel fābulārum vocābulīs novīs adhibitīs:** once students have progressed past the first chapters they may be asked to compose sentences or a story using the new vocabulary introduced in each chapter. This may be done *ad libitum* or on the basis of a projected image.

TESTING

With other approaches to Latin teaching students may fall behind and yet escape notice because their comprehension and preparation may not be immediately apparent. The instructor may believe that he is teaching when little in fact is being learned. The ancients understood, however, that *doctrīna* and *disciplīna* are inseparable; since more learning takes place in the classroom, and since the fruits of study are more immediately apparent, the teacher using *LINGUA LATINA PER SE ILLUSTRATA* should have little trouble monitoring an individual student's progress. For this reason formal testing may not always be as necessary. Prof. Thomson points out four ways that the teacher can monitor students's progress on a continual basis:

(a) By making individuals read parts of the passage aloud in a manner which shows understanding through correct phrasing and intonation. (If the passage contains dialogue, different students will take the parts, with the teacher, perhaps, acting as narrator; the best students should not always be chosen, but mixed in, apparently at random, with weaker ones, who will draw strength from the competition.) In many cases this simple check will be all that is necessary, but it is not always reliable and it does not test everyone in the class.

(b) By asking questions in simple Latin about the content of the passage just read (suggestions for such questions are found in the *EXERCITIA LATINA*). These may be accompanied by the showing of pictures. When answering, students may be allowed to keep their books open, so that if necessary they can find an appropriate answer in the text. The fact that they can find the right answer shows that they have understood both question and answer. If the student replies in English, the teacher should smile encouragingly and say *"Latīnē!"* or *"Respondē Latīnē!"*

(c) By asking questions in simple Latin or in English and instructing students to answer in English (*"Respondē Anglicē!"*). Some teachers may find this a dangerous procedure, since it may encourage students to be conscious of an English substratum beneath the Latin. It can be useful, but it should be used sparingly. The same is true of asking students for an English paraphrase of a lengthy passage of Latin. This should never be done except in an oral teacher-led activity.

(d) By giving special manipulation exercises, orally or in writing, like those in the *EXERCITIA LATINA*, to check and secure comprehension of new material as it occurs in the narrative text. These include the filling in of inflexional endings or missing words in a context which usually demands only one right choice, the completion of unfinished sentences, and the techniques of substitution and transformation.

Exercises which interrupt the narrative should be conducted with reasonable dispatch, so that the story line does not become buried beneath a mass of grammatical and other minutiae...The questions in *Pensum C* may be answered by complete Latin sentences or by a Latin word or phrase, provided that the appropriate grammatical forms are given (e.g. *Quem Iūlius audit? — Mārcum.*)

One final caveat: Students are not always aware that they have not really understood something, and even if they are, they will sometimes hesitate to admit it. Teachers must therefore ask searching questions, look for students who seem bewildered, bored, or withdrawn, and create an atmosphere in which slow learners are not afraid to ask questions.

Nonetheless, any classroom setting will demand formal means of testing students's progress. Students must always be aware of what they are expected to learn and what degree of assimilation is required. This should be fairly straightforward, since testing will generally be based on the same kinds of exercises they have been doing in class.

Instructor will develop their own testing techniques corresponding to their own teaching style. Tests may simply consist of the *Pēnsa* for each chapter, they may repeat *Exercitia* and other material done in class, or they may demand more free composition. Professor Martha Davis, recipient of the American Philological Association award for distinguished teaching, has used *LINGUA LATINA PER SE ILLUSTRATA* at Temple University for many years with great success. She divides her tests and quizzes into four parts. *Pars prīma* tests rote memorization, concentrating on principal parts of the "top 50" verbs (see Appendix VI) and then on noun and adjective declensions. Vocabulary and any other material for memorization might also be included in *pars prīma*. *Pars altera* involves the manipulation of forms. Students may be asked to write in Latin, to "reverse" forms (changing from singular to plural or vice versa), to change voice from active to passive, from one tense to another or from one mood to another. *Pars tertia* consists of parsing: identifying forms and syntax of individual words in a passage which may be underlined or listed separately below the citation. *Pars quārta* involves translation from Latin to English. About half of these passages they have already studied, the other half are passages of comparable difficulty for sight translation.

SOME GENERAL RECOMMENDATIONS

1. Vocabulary

The course LINGVA LATINA PER SE ILLVSTRATA contains about 4,000 words. The words presented in the text have not been chosen arbitrarily but rather on the basis of the best frequency lists of classical Latin vocabulary.[17] It has been demonstrated that the 1,600 words choosen by frequency constitute 80% of the vocabulary of the ancient Latin corpus of texts. They thus constitute the basic vocabulary for the texts of the classical authors. Grammar/translation approaches do not give enough time to the learning of vocabulary, and are therefore obliged to rely heavily on artificial means such as flash cards and word lists. In the LINGVA LATINA PER SE ILLVSTRATA course, on the contrary, acquiring vocabulary is considered fundamental, and the texts are structured so as to facilitate its assimilation through calculated repetition of the words in different contexts, vocabulary exercises, and stimulation of the inductive process for understanding the meaning of new words. It is absolutely essential that the teacher verify the perfect assimilation of vocabulary on the part of the students, who must learn all the words of the course, and not only passively but also in such a manner as to be able to use them when opportune. The best way to definitively fix words in the memory is to use them in meaningful situations. Contextualization provides a series of mnemonic supports which permit the student to memorize words and retain them more easily.

Mastering a substantial vocabulary is a *condiciō sine quā nōn* for fluent reading of classical texts; during the first two years of study this should be achieved without use of a dictionary. In the teaching of Latin and Greek the strange idea has become prevalent that a dictionary should be used in the first stages of language learning, to be put aside at a more advanced stage. An effective pedagogy, however, is based on the opposite approach: frequent use of the dictionary belongs to an advanced stage of language learning, when the basic vocabulary has already been acquired.[18] At the elementary level the dictionary should not be the normal instrument of study, since it both wastes time and creates the habit of translation into English. Basic vocabulary should be learned by associating words with things, and not with words in another language. Naturally this approach can only be adopted when—as in the LINGVA LATINA PER SE ILLVSTRATA course—the primary texts are composed in such a way as to gradually augment vocabulary in a rational manner, rather than listing desultory collections of words which present students with no prospect of making sense of them on their own. Flash-cards may still be helpful in learning vocabulary, and the index of the 208 most common principal parts in the booklet GRAMMATICA LATINA p. 23 ff. may be assigned for memorization, especially with upper level students. But even this work of rote memorization will be greatly eased by the experience of recognizing these words in context. Only when the lexical foundation has been acquired and fully assimilated is it practical for students to make use of a dictionary to find suggestions for a more elegant and efficient rendering of what the student has already understood in Latin, when called on to make a literary translation.

2. Students must know what is expected of them

At all levels students should have a clear idea of what preparation is expected of them. Preteen students will do most of their learning directly in the classroom; older students can be expected to prepare more on their own. Prof. Thomson makes the following remarks about assignments for college and university students; his advice may be adapted depending on the maturity of secondary level students.

No two students prepare work exactly alike, and allowance must be made for individual differences, but the teacher may suggest the following steps as a guide:

(a) Reread the material covered in the previous lesson. This will refresh your memory of what you have already learned, and prime you for the next step.

(b) Study any illustrations that accompany the new assignment, bearing in mind that their only purpose is to help you understand the Latin you are about to read. Do not try to describe in words what you see, but note the persons, objects, or action depicted. If a Latin caption goes with the illustration—let your eye rove between the two. It may help to read the caption, then close your eyes and imagine the illustration, and vice versa.

(c) Read the entire assignment through aloud until you have some idea of its general sense. Never try to put any of it into English. Try to sense what words seem to belong together — careful attention to punctuation will help — and what intonations to give individual words and phrases. (*Note to teacher:* Many students will have difficulties in doing this successfully. The teacher, in giving out the assignment, may tell the students where the junctures occur, and have them mark these in pencil with slash marks.)

(d) Read the assignment again, sentence by sentence. If a clear mental picture forms as you read, go on to the next sentence. Tackle any difficulties positively, and do not be contented with failure. First consult the marginalia and the context itself, remembering that they provide good clues to

---

17   v., in particular, P. B. Diederich, *The Frequency of Latin Words and Their Endings*, The University of Chicago Press, Chicago, Illinois, 1939; G. Lodge, *The Vocabulary of High School Latin,* Teachers Coll., New York, 1907; L. Delatte, Et. Evrard, S. Govaerts, J. Denooz, *Dictionnaire fréquentiel et index inverse de la langue latine,* L. A. S. L. A. (Laboratoire d'analyse statistique des langues anciennes), Université de Liège, 1981; Maurice Mathy, *Vocabulaire de base du latin,* Editions O. C. D. L., Paris VIIe, 1952; *A Basic Latin Vocabulary,* published for the Orbilian Society by Centaur Books, 4th impression 1956 (1st impression 1949); D. Gardner, *Frequency Dictionary of Classical Latin Words*, Stanford University, 1971; G. Cauquil-J.Y. Guillaumin, *Vocabulaire de base du latin* (alphabétique, fréquentiel, étymologique), Besançon, ARELAB, 1984; E. Riganti, Lessico latino fondamentale, Pàtron, Bologna, 1989.

18   The best introductory level Latin dictionary is the *Elementary Latin Dictionary* by C.T. Lewis (Oxford, 1998). Also useful is the *Latin Concise Dictionary* which includes English-Latin entries (HarperCollins, 2003.) No advanced student will want to be without *Smith's English-Latin Dictionary* by W. Smith and T.D. Hall (Bolchazy-Carducci, 2000.)

the meaning of the word or phrase which is holding you up. Then read the Latin again until a clear and distinct image rises from the Latin words. If you are satisfied that you have made your best effort, but the meaning is still unclear, underline the difficult part lightly in pencil, and pay particular attention when it is dealt with in class. When the difficulty has been removed, erase the pencil mark.

The teacher should vigorously discourage the writing of English words between the lines of the Latin text, and the persistent use of a Latin-English lexicon. No reward should be forthcoming for anything but reliance on native ingenuity and the clues provided by the textbook and the teacher. Questions about English words derived from Latin are in order and should be answered, but the use of English should play no part in the students' preparation.

3. Motivating students

One of the most important conditions for learning is that the student be animated by a strong motivation. Many teachers are convinced that students of today, distracted by too many other interests far removed from their studies, are incapable of such motivation for Latin studies. But the success of American high school teachers in attracting students over the last twenty years shows how much can be achieved if teachers are willing to appeal to students with some degree of savvy. It is often not difficult to infect thirteen or fourteen-year-old youngsters—and even younger students—with an enthusiasm for the conquest of new and unexplored worlds that possession of a language like Latin can open up for them. Naturally an indispensable factor for the students's emotional engagement is the success of the learning process. In using *LINGVA LATINA PER SE ILLVSTRATA* they will recognize that their efforts achieve corresponding results, especially when these results are recognized in a gratifying manner. The so-called Pygmalion effect, which can have disastrous results when a teacher forms a negative opinion of a student, can be applied to constructive effect when students, continually encouraged by their teacher, are stimulated to conserve a positive sense of their own potential, and find their daily progress palpable. Students' enthusiasm increases as if by contagion as they marvel at their ability to understand increasingly difficult texts, and thereby daily gain confidence in themselves and their abilities. One should not be grudging in praising one's students, while at the same time not devaluing compliments by awarding them left and right. One should above all emphasize the students' successes in overcoming obstacles, and not make too much of their mistakes. This is not to say, of course, that one should neglect to scrupulously correct mistakes, but rather that such correction should be done without punitive intent and with the confidence that students can achieve better results. The teacher's manifest affection for the students will make the classroom a joyful place and not a place of misery. The students should be stimulated with exercises and questions skillfully calibrated so that they are neither so difficult as to cause frustration, nor so simple as to diminish students' concentration and interest. This capacity to motivate students will be a direct function of the teacher's love for them; the Augustinian *dīlige, et quod vīs fac* applies also to teaching.

4. Communicate confidence to the students

The teacher should never show discouragement, doubts, or indecision. The teacher should always have a very clear idea of what he intends to achieve in each class, and should be vigilant not to show any uncertainty. At the beginning students will have some difficulty in the automatic use of the case system, which is very different from the normal structure of our language. An inexperienced teacher may be discouraged by this, lose confidence in the success of his teaching, and communicate this uncertainty to the students. One can solve these problems by giving the students more time, giving them more exercises, having them read, speak, and write. It is best not to proceed until one is certain that the students possess the system of declensions to the point of being able to use the appropriate cases in the right place without having to stop and think. If one always maintains the initial enthusiasm and conducts class with vigor and confidence, never losing certainty of a successful outcome, these expectations will not be disappointed.

5. Grammar

A teacher using *LINGVA LATINA PER SE ILLVSTRATA* for the first time may have the sense that grammar plays a marginal role in the course, and is not considered important. This impression is entirely false: grammar and the conscious learning of the mechanisms that govern the operation of language is as fundamental in this course as in those that follow the grammar/translation approach. The difference consists rather in the sequence in which the rules of language are presented. The inductive principle underlying the course foresees that rules will first be encountered in context and then systematically confirmed. The teacher should therefore avoid anticipating material that might only confuse the minds of students, and instead assemble the pieces of the mosaic one by one. In grammar/translation courses the rule is presented abstractly, then practiced with a dozen sentences, and not encountered again for some time, by when the student may have forgotten it through lack of use. In *LINGVA LATINA PER SE ILLVSTRATA,* by contrast, the rule or form continues to play an important role in the student's reading after it has been first encountered, discussed, and learned. The first lessons, for example, do not speak yet of the "first" or "second" declension, but only of "masculine," "feminine," and "neuter" nouns and the corresponding adjectival forms. The concept of "declension" will only be introduced in chapter IX, with the presentation of parisyllabic and imparisyllabic third declension nouns. *Nōmina dēclīnāre et verba in prīmīs puerī sciant: neque enim aliter pervenīre ad intellēctum sequentium possunt*[19]: the ancient advice of Quintilian naturally applies also to our own students. By *dēclīnāre* he means knowing how to use the correct form in the right place, so as to be capable of recognizing it without possibility of error in one's reading.

The teacher should thus be prepared to present new constructions and structures as they are introduced. This entails reading the chapter in advance, studying it carefully together with the *LATINE DISCO* and organizing the class in such a way that all the phenomena encountered will appear as clearly as possible to the students, leaving no uncertainties. In subsequent lessons the instructor must verify that these points have been completely assimilated, and decide when to interpose more detailed study of them, perhaps with reference to *SYNTAXIS LATINA*. In no case should one settle for a vague and approximate understanding on the part of the students, content that they understand the material "more or less." *Omnia ad unguem*—only when students have achieved an exact and rigorous command of Latin can the teacher be satisfied of having fully exploited *LINGVA LATINA PER SE ILLVSTRATA*.

---

19   Quint., 1, 4, 22.

NOTES FOR THE INSTRUCTOR NOT INCLUDED IN THE STUDENT'S MANUAL *LATINE DISCO*

It has already been pointed out that the students's manual *LATINE DISCO* is, irrespective of its title, as useful to the instructor as to the student of *LINGVA LATINA PER SE ILLVSTRATA*. The teacher and home-school parent can best plan their lessons by following the outlines there proposed. New points of grammar are summarized in the margins, aligned next to passages of text that explain them. Since it is advisable that home-school parents work through the course together with their children, their first resource in working through the chapters should be the student's manual *LATINE DISCO*.

Pious reticence demands the omission from *LATINE DISCO* of some points, perhaps useful for the instructor, that might only confuse the student. Such material is presented below; points already discussed in *LATINE DISCO* are not touched on here. The notes below are directed to teachers, but also represent an effort to make the structure of the course intelligible to home-school parents. They include suggestions on how to teach the material as well as points of information. Of course such suggestions are not prescriptions, since the books can be taught successfully in a variety of ways, according to the temperament and strengths of teacher and students.

The notes on the first *lēctiō* of *Capitulum I* are more extensive because they represent a pattern that can be applied to other *capitula*; they are a variation on material presented in the section "Planning a typical lesson" above and in Appendices I and II. The reader may forgive any redundancy on the grounds that *repetīta iuvant*.

A few general points, beginning with a reiteration of two points already touched on:

- While teaching *FAMILIA ROMANA* the teacher may be tempted to introduce exceptions, qualify rules, introduce paradigms or other material not yet explicitly covered in the text. Teachers used to the grammar/translation method are particularly vulnerable to this temptation, which should generally be resisted. For reasons discussed more fully above, it is pedagogically more effective to observe the principle of pious reticence and teach only the material that is covered in each *lectio* and *capitulum*.

- Another temptation that may beset the teacher is that of going too fast. *Omnis festinatio a diabolo*. In this respect a characteristic virtue of *LINGUA LATINA PER SE ILLUSTRATA* also represents a danger. Precisely because the levels are so subtly graded, it is often possible to move on to new *capitula* before having fully mastered a previous one. Sooner or later, however, such haste will retard the students's progress. If students begin to find the material introduced in a new *capitulum* difficult, it is a sure sign that the class has moved too quickly. The class should not proceed until all students have fully mastered each *capitulum*; that means being able to answer the *exercitia*, *pensa* or other extemporaneous questions on its contents spontaneously and without reference to any written notes. *Non multa sed multum*.

- Thus the teacher or parent will have in each case to determine the appropriate pace for a class or individual student, neither moving so quickly as to preclude the necessary full assimilation of the subject matter, nor so slowly as to bore the better students. Here, as generally, *est modus in rēbus*.

- The declensions are presented in an order that may be new to some American readers. The nominative is directly followed by the accusative instead of the genitive. This is the order preferred by linguists, since the accusative is closest in form to the nominative. It also serves to put the oblique cases in contrast to the nominative *cāsus rēctus* (the vocative case is not listed, since it is only exceptionally different from the nominative). When new words are introduced, however, and in the *Index vocabulōrum*, their genitive singular form is given together with the nominative and the gender of the noun—the three pieces of essential information which the student must memorize in order to decline the noun properly. By the time whole paradigms are presented students will already have encountered its different forms in context. For example, the first and second declension noun paradigms do not appear until the end of *Capitulum VIII*, but students have been dealing with forms of these declensions since the beginning of the book. Once students are familiar with the declensions new words are presented in the margins (as in the INDICES) in both nominative and genitive forms, so that the student can immediately learn the declension and the stem of the noun. The memorization of paradigms, however necessary, is facilitated by this contextual introduction. Students should be capable of generating all noun forms without reference to a paradigm.

- The principal parts of verbs are given in the following order: present active infinitive; perfect active infinitive; supine ending in *-um*, not in *-tum*. Third conjugation *-io* verbs can be recognized by the insertion of an *-io* after the present infinitive in the paradigm. Students should memorize the principal parts of all verbs they have encountered; from these forms they should be able to spontaneously generate all forms of the verbs they have encountered. A list of the most important principal parts for memorization is contained in the blue booklet *GRAMMATICA LATINA*.

- Both *LATINE DISCO* and the following notes generally refer only to the first occurrence of a grammatical form or syntactical structure. Once encountered, however, these forms and structures recur in the text with a calculated frequency. The teacher should not hesitate to bring attention to these repetitions so as to ensure that every student in the class has complete command of the form or rule in question. One common defect of grammar/translation texts is that a rule or form may be introduced and practiced in drills, but not encountered again in continuous reading for some time. The more often the student recognizes a rule or form in context, the better it is learned.

Capitulum I: IMPERIUM ROMANUM singular and plural numbers 85-106; interrogatives *est, -ne, num, ubi, quid*; ablative with *in;* letters and numerals

Lēctiō prīma (1-22)

The very first lines of this first *capitulum* show students how they can learn Latin in Latin. This process, called contextual induction, seems little different from the way students has learned their mother tongue, albeit more concentrated and efficient. The teacher will bolster students' confidence and enthusiasm by making them aware of this.

In conducting class an overhead projector, always useful, is especially helpful at these beginning stages. A transparency of the map should first be projected on the screen. The teacher should say the place names out loud and point to them on the screen; this can be done entirely in Latin. With very young students (7-9 years old) it is useful to ask them to come to the screen to point out specific places. The teacher might ask e.g. *Ubi est Rōma?* Once students understand the question they eagerly volunteer to identify place names on the map. Older students already familiar with the geography will still be interested to learn the Latin place names.

A transparency of the first page of *Capitulum Prīmum* may then be projected on the screen. The teacher should introduce the material by reading the first paragraph out loud, slowly, clearly, and intelligibly; the students should then read the same material out loud, in choral fashion. Choral repetition encourages all students, even the most shy, to speak out loud. Students may then volunteer to read the passage out loud individually; the younger the students are, the more important that they develop this habit of reading out loud from the beginning.

Already in the first lines students should be led to discover for themselves the relation between the singular form *est* and the plural *sunt*. Next they discover the meaning of the word *quoque*. Here, as throughout the course, the teacher should resist the temptation to blurt out the meaning in English, but instead pose leading questions and give sufficient examples that even students who have not immediately recognized its meaning can do so. This can be done entirely in Latin.

When working with younger students it is best to proceed one paragraph at a time. Even with adult students it is best not to read the whole *lēctiō* at once; there is a great deal of new material to be absorbed. A single class period should never cover more than a single *lēctiō*; this first *lēctiō* ends at line 22. Cognitive psychologists suggest that students should not normally be exposed to new material for more than 45 seconds at a time without some kind of repetition or interrogation.

By the time students have reached line 15 they will be able to respond to a range of questions in Latin. Students should be led to discover for themselves that the suffix *-ne* introduces a type of question—one that can be answered yes or no—different from the type of question introduced by the interrogative *ubi*. Although the material is entirely new to them, students will be excited to see how much they can understand for themselves. It is helpful for the teacher to pose many questions spontaneously in Latin, on the model of the questions in the text. It is best to address these questions to as many different students as possible, taking care not to introduce vocabulary or constructions that have not yet appeared in the text. The equivalent of "yes" in responding to a Latin question is *ita* or *sic*, while the contrary answer is *minimē*; The student can also respond by repeating the whole sentence e.g.: *Estne Nīlus insula? Nīlus nōn est insula*, or, more simply: *Non est. Estne Tusculum oppidum? Est.*

After thus going over the *lectiō* closely it may be effective for the teacher to give the students five minutes to study the text silently, reading it over to themselves at least three times. The intensity of their preparation will be increased by the awareness that they will soon be questioned about the material. Students are then asked to close their books, and the instructor questions them in Latin about the *lectiō* they have prepared. Here again it will be helpful to refer to an overhead transparency with an image of the map. The students should be able to respond spontaneously and accurately to any questions about the reading, to the extent that they have virtually memorized the *lectiō*. In interrogating students the teacher may refer to his own text, but questions will be more rapid and effective if the teacher has also committed the material to memory.

Students may then prepare the questions in *EXERCITIA LATINA* corresponding to the first *lectiō, exercitia* 1-3 on p. 7, if the teacher has not found it opportune to use them at an earlier stage. For example, if students are having trouble grasping the difference between *est* and *sunt* the teacher might choose to go over the first *exercitium* even before completing the *lectiō*. Preparing the *exercitia* means being able to spontaneously give a correct answer without reference to any writing on paper or in one's book.

It is advisable that students be forbidden from writing in their books, since this serves as a crutch and prevents them from repeating the exercises. If the *exercitia* are to be assigned as written homework it is better that they be written out separately.

The teacher should be confident that all students have an active mastery of each *lēctiō*, and *ā fortiōrī* of each *capitulum*, before moving on to the next one. Even after moving on it will be useful to frequently review prior *lēctiōnēs* and *capitula* by interrogating the students in Latin with reference to the corresponding overhead transparency, such as the map *Imperium Rōmānum* from this *capitulum*. A complete set of transparencies with the Peer Lauritzen illustrations for the separate *capitula* of *FAMILIA ROMANA* is available from Focus Publishing.

The procedure here described for teaching this first *lēctiō* can be applied, with suitable variations, to all subsequent *lēctiōnēs*.

The homeschooling parent should likewise be sure that the student is capable of answering all the *exercitia* spontaneously and correctly before moving on to the next *lectiō*. The parent who does not know Latin may want to keep a copy of the answer keys (entitled *pēnsa solūta* and *exercitia solūta*) at hand to check the accuracy of the student's work.

Lēctiō secunda (22-61)

Adjectives: the singular and plural forms of the adjectives are presented in all three genders. It is not necessary for students to know that they are learning the first and second declensions forms, or even that the different forms they are encountering are masculine, feminine, and neuter. It is, however, essential, that they recognize and be able to form the singular and plural forms of the three nouns *fluvius, īnsula,* and *oppidum* (pictured on p. 7) and their corresponding adjectives. Note that the second pair of adjectives here introduced, *pauci* and *multi,* will not be used in the singular in *FAMILIA ROMANA.*

The sense of the interrogative *num* can be conveyed by raising intonation to show that the question expects a negative response.

Lēctiō tertia (62-83)

Letters and numbers: the correct pronunciation of the letters and numbers is given in the marginal notes.

Here more nouns *(numerus, littera, vocābulum)* are introduced, following *prōvincia* in the previous *lectiō;* students can generate the plural forms by analogy with the three nouns learned in *lectiō secunda.*

Lēctiō grammatica (84-106)

Here the concept of number—singular and plural—which students have been dealing with throughout this *capitulum,* is formally explained. This section should be as closely studied as the other *lectiōnes,* though the grammatical concepts will be very easy since the students have already applied them in practice. *Exercitium* 11 corresponding to this *Lēctiō grammatica* should also be prepared.

Pēnsa

As the *exercitia* repeat the material in each *lēctiō,* so the *pēnsa* resume the *capitulum* as a whole. *Pēnsum A* and *B* are substitution drills, the first covering new terminations and forms, the second covering new vocabulary. *Pensum C* requires the generation of whole sentences in response to specific questions. The class should not move on to the next *capitulum* until all students are capable of answering the *Pēnsa* with ease and without reference to prepared notes.

Colloquium

The blue book entitled *COLLOQUIA PERSONARUM* presents useful and enjoyable review of the material contained in *capitula I-XXIV.* As *colloquia* or dialogues they lend themselves to student participation, and class will be livelier if students act out these *colloquia* in front of the class occasionally. The material may be prepared or read at sight after completion of the *capitulum.* Classes using the Late Latin or ecclesiastical pronunciation may want to skip *Colloquium I,* since it presupposes use of the restored pronunciation.

Capitulum II: FAMILIA ROMANA *prōnōmina possessīva meus/ tuus 66-79,* masculine, feminine, neuter genders 95-105; *cāsus*

genetīvus 105-211; genetīvus + numbers 47, 56; interrogatives *quis, quae, qui, cuius, quot;* numeral endings;

Lēctiō prīma (1-24)

Grammars generally present the feminine form of the interrogative pronoun as *quis,* identical with the masculine, and identify the form *quae* with the relative pronoun. For pedagogical reasons Ørberg here (line 16) prefers to give the feminine form of the interrogative as *quae,* a form which actually occurs in classical usage. Depending on the age and background of the students the teacher may here want to point out that the form *quis* does in fact sometimes occur as the feminine of the interrogative pronoun, as in Plautus: *Quis est ea quam vīs dūcere uxōrem? (Aulul. 170); Quis illaec est mulier quae ipsa sē miseratur? (Epid. 533).*

In this chapter the concept of declension has not yet been introduced. The student reads in *LATINE DISCO* that nouns ending in *-us* are masculine, those ending in *-a* feminine. Every teacher knows that this general principle needs to be qualified. It is enough to think of *mālus, pirus,* and other names of trees and plants, or of *methodus* and other nouns derived from Greek for the second declension; of *nauta, poēta,* and other masculine nouns of the first declension. But these are exceptions to the rule, and at this stage of learning pious reticence demands that students focus on the rule itself. The exceptions will appear in due course.

Lēctiō secunda (25-62)

This lectio introduces the genitive case, the case of possession. The interrogative pronoun *cuius* is useful to the teacher in questioning students. The instructor can give substitution drills by asking students to restate *magnus/parvus numerus* + the genitive in terms of *multi/pauci* and vice versa, as in *exercitium* 8 on p. 11. The teachers should give special attention that students learn the masculine, feminine and neuter forms of the numbers *duo* and *tres* given in the margins.

Lēctiō tertia (63-92)

The noun *liber* introduced in this *lēctiō* (line 81) appears first in its plural form *librī,* which students can contrast with the word *līberī* which they met in the first *lēctiō* of this *capitulum* (line 21). Throughout the course nouns with similar spellings but different vowel quantities will be juxtaposed, reminding students that the macron is an essential part of a word's spelling—words that may look identical can have very different meanings! The teacher can use the possessive pronouns *meus* and *tuus* introduced in this *lēctiō* in posing the students questions like those in the dialogue between Cornelius and Julius.

Capitulum III: PUER IMPROBUS *prōnōmen relātīvum 69-82,* nominative/accusative cases 84-97; verbs (present indicative); nominative and accusative of personal pronouns; interrogative and relative pronouns; *Cur...? Quia...*

Lēctiō prīma (1-21)

This action-packed *capitulum* introduces the temporal verb and the accusative case. An overhead transparency is particularly useful in illustrating the sequence of events. It is a measure of Ørberg's meticulous fidelity that even the exclamations here used—*"Lalla," "st," "fu," tuxtas,"*etc.— are attested in classical sources.

Lēctiō secunda (22-48)

The teacher may point out the long vowel quantity indicated by the macron over the adverb *hīc* (line 41); this will aid students to distinguish this word from the pronoun *hic* which they will soon encounter.

Lēctiō tertia (49-82)

Students ignorant of the distinction between the pronominal forms *who* and *whom* may be hard pressed to distinguish between *qui* and *quem*. Resort may be had to the vernacular if it helps the students understand this important distinction, e.g. "The girl *whom* Marcus hits is Julia." These passages exercising the relative and interrogative pronouns should give the teacher occasion to drill students on the use of relative constructions in the accusative or nominative cases. Students may be given two separate sentences, and asked to combine them into a single sentence with a relative clause. E.g. *Iūlia Aemiliam vocat. Aemilia est māter līberōrum.* □*Aemilia quam Iūlia vocat est māter līberōrum. Exercitia 6-9* in *Exercitia Latina* provide excellent review and may be done repeatedly.

Lēctiō grammatica (83-118)

For the first time students here encounter the form of the basic phrase: subject + object + verb.

Capitulum IV: DOMINUS ET SERVI prōnōmina possessīva suus 19, vocative case; indicative and imperative moods (106-121); genitives of *is, ea, id; eius/suum; numerī 9-10*

Lēctiō prīma (1-43)

Here the imperative mood and the vocative case are encountered. The teacher should see to it that students thoroughly learn the cardinal numbers from one to ten (9-10). Number drills can be done by going around the room and having each student in turn count a number out loud. Addition drills such as that in *exercitium 2* are also useful. For the first time students meet compounds of the verb *esse*, as indicated in the marginal notes (20-23).

Lēctiō secunda (44-98)

Although composed of three scenes, this chapter is divided into only two *lēctiōnēs*. This second *lēctiō* introduces the reciprocal pronoun *suus-a-um*, which must be carefully distinguished from *eius* and the possessive adjectives *meus/tuus. Exercitium 5* provides excellent review. In line 75 *quod*, the neuter of the relative pronoun, is introduced for the first time. The complete pronoun declensions will be given at the end of *capitulum VIII*, by which time all forms will have been encountered.

Capitulum V: VILLA ET HORTUS accusative case; ablative with prepositions; complete declension of *is, ea, id; ablātīvus locī, ablātīvus comitātūs, ablātīvus sēparātīvus/ ēgestātis; praepositiōnēs + abl. 136; imperātīvus 139-156, numerus singulāris/plūrālis verbī 139-156*

Lēctiō prīma (1-46)

This *lēctiō* introduces the accusative plural and the ablative. The ablatives with *in, cum* and *sine* are called the *ablātīvus locī, ablātīvus comitātūs* and *ablātīvus sēparātīvus* or

ēgestātis respectively.

Lēctiō secunda (47-105)

Here students meet the plural of the imperative and more plural forms of the indicative. The uses of *ab* and *ex* here introduced are two more examples of the *ablātīvus sēparātīvus*.

Note the juxtaposition of the verb *rīdēre* used intransitively in line 69 (*Mārcus et Quīntus rīdent*) and transitively in the next line (*"Puerī etiam mē rīdent!"*) In line 85 *hīc* has not a spatial but a temporal sense, indicating the moment at hand.

Capitulum VI: VIA LATINA prepositions with accusative 97-107 and ablative; ***Ubi/Quō…?***; city names; active/passive voices; ***cāsus locātīvus (114-115, 120-121); ablātīvus īnstrūmentī, ablātīvus agentis; passīvum 122-139; praepositiō 97-109, praepositiōnēs 97-107, passīvum 122-139;***

Lēctiō prīma (1-45)

Students learn comparisons with *tam…quam* and prepositions with the accusative in relation to the Roman road system. It is important that students become familiar with irregular forms such as *it/eunt* (lines 20-21) and learn them perfectly.

Lēctiō secunda (46-95)

The archaic interrogatives "whence" and "whither" may help students understand these three words asking "where?" Many questions can be devised with *quō, ubi, unde*. The passive voice is introduced in line 62 together with the *ablātīvus agentis*. The student now knows two very different uses of the preposition *ā/ab*: the *ablātīvus agentis* and the *ablātīvus sēparātīvus*. The teacher may want to give transformation drills from the active to passive voices and vice versa, like those in *exercitium 8*. Although *via, porta, pōns*, etc. are generally used in the ablative case to indicate route (the *ablātīvus itineris*, really a form of the *ablātīvus īnstrūmentī*), in line 76 *per* and the accusative is used to avoid repetition of the ablative: *Quī viā Latīnā venit per portam Capēnam Rōmam intrat.* Cf. Livy (33. 26.9): *Lupus Esquilīnā portā ingressus, Tūscō vīcō atque inde per portam Capēnam prope intāctus ēvāserat.* For other examples of such *variatio* see Livy 4.46.6; 23.47.8. Note how the examples *Rōmae* and *Tūsculī*, juxtaposed in line 47, fix in the student's mind the correct formation of the locative (in *Cap. XXV* they will learn *Athēnīs*).

Capitulum VII: PUELLA ET ROSA dative case; the reflexive *sē; Nonne…est? Num…est? plēnus + genitīvus; hic haec hoc (43, 85, 90)*

Treatment of the dative case in this chapter completes the introduction of the case system.

Lēctiō prīma (1-29)

Having met *hīc* in *Capitulum III*, the students now encounter *illīc* in line 3; gradually all the spatial adverbs will be introduced. These two adverbs lead to the pronominal forms *hic* and *ille* in the next *capitulum*. The difference between *in* with the accusative and the ablative, juxtaposed in lines 14-15 and well illustrated by the marginal illustration, is the same as that between the English prepositions *into* and *in*. In-class commands may be useful in insuring that students can recognize and use the imperatives of the verb *esse* given in the margin of line 23.

This *lēctiō* is an opportunity to return to the important distinction between *suus* and *eius*: cf. lines 3, 4, 7, 10, 28 and *exercitium 3*. The reciprocal sense of *suus*, "one's own," should be stressed. This distinction can be reviewed by discussing *Colloquium V: Num Mēdus nummōs suōs numerat?*

Lēctiō secunda (30-60)

Note the significant difference in vowel quantity between the word *mālum*, introduced in line 41, and the adjective *malus-a-um* introduced in the previous *capitulum* at line 39. The teacher may point out that virtually the same distinction exists between *sē* and *eum/eam*, *eōs/eās* as between *suus* and *eius*. This is evident in a comparison of lines 14-15: (*Syra ōstium aperit et in cubiculum intrat, neque ōstium post sē claudit.*) with lines 34-36 (*Dominus per ōstium in vīllam intrat. Post eum veniunt Syrus et Lēander... Ōstiārius post eōs ōstium claudit.*) It is not opportune at this point to point out that *inest*, which appears first in line 39, can also govern a simple dative case, like many other verbs compounded with a preposition. This possibility will be shown further on when the dative is covered in greater detail, or it may be mentioned when students encounter the following phrase in *Capitulum IX* (line 84): *Pāstor laetus ovem in umerōs impōnit.* As apparent from the usage in line 43, *plēnus* in classical Latin governs the genitive more often than the ablative. The teacher may choose to point out that *plēnus mālōrum* could be substituted for by *plēnus mālīs*; if so, when constructions of *plēnus* with the genitive are later encountered the teacher may ask students to give the equivalent construction with the ablative.

Lēctiō tertia (61-104)

In line 76 students encounter the imperative of the verb *īre*. It is important that students learn these forms. Instruction in use of the imperatives can be an occasion for memorable in-class demonstrations! Students have now met all dative forms, including those of *quī, quae, quod*, and *quis, quae, quid* in line 101. The pronouns will be treated systematically in the next chapter.

Capitulum VIII: *TABERNA ROMANA* pronouns (relative, interrogative, demonstrative), *ablātīvus instrumentī, ablātīvus pretiī, prōnōmen relatīvum quis/quī quae quid/quod 135-211, prōnōmina dēmōnstrātīva ille-a-ud (135-211); prōnōmina interrogātīva quis/quī (135-211), is, ea, id (135-211); prōnōmina dēmōnstrātīva hic 212-223*

Lēctiō prīma (1-35)

(3) The elision of the demonstrative in the same gender, number, and case as the relative is immediately comprehensible for the masculine singular, although less for for the feminine and the plural as in lines 14, 16, 101, cf. 35

(122) Make sure that students have correctly understood *aliī... aliī = some...others* from the context.

(33) Underline the ending *-ud* of the neuter of *alius*, like that of the neuter form of *ille* (l. 79).

Lēctiō secunda (36-82)

(56) In discussing the ablative of price one may point out that the genitive of value is used with the forms *tantī* and *quantī*. The same is true of *plūris* and *minōris*, which they will not encounter for a while. Practice questions may be asked in class

such as: *Quantī cōnstat...?, Quantī stat...?, Ānulus Lȳdiae tantī stat quantī ānulus Aemiliae, Ānulus cum gemmā plūris cōnstat quam ānulus sine gemmā* etc. The general guiding principle of the course, of course, is not to present forms and structures which have not yet been encountered in context, but an occasional anticipation or development of a point touched on in the reading may not be harmful, so long as it does not become a general rule. It is fundamental, however, to practice the material under study both orally and in writing as frequently as possible.

Lēctiō tertia (83-133)

Lēctiō grammatica (134-223)

The grammar section in this *capitulum* is worth special attention, because it provides a comprehensive review of the pronoun forms which must be thoroughly learned, both in context and in the paradigm forms given for *hic, haec, hoc* (the other pronoun paradigms appear in the index on p. 308.) It is important to take the time to make sure that students have so thoroughly memorized these paradigms that they can apply them readily.

Capitulum IX: *PASTOR ET OVES dēclīnātiō prīma (89-99) et secunda, dēclīnātiō tertia*

Lēctiō prīma (1-38)

Note the juxtaposition of two verbs with a significant difference in vowel quantity in line 11: *ēst* and *est*. *Ūndēcentum* in line 3 is found in Pliny the Elder (7.60.60 §214), and Valerius Maximus uses *ūndēcentēsimus* (8.7.11) which supposes *ūndēcentum*. The form *nōnāgintā novem* can also be found, as in the famous Gospel passage: *Quis ex vōbīs homō, quī habet centum ovēs, et sī perdiderit ūnam ex illīs, nōnne dīmittit nōnāgintā novem in dēsertō et vādit ad illam quae perierat, dōnec inveniat eam?*(Luc. 15, 4-5) Likewise the number can be written either IC or XCIX.

Lēctiō secunda (39-86)

The verb *petere* appears first with the meaning "to head for" (32-33, 41, 47, 80) but then (74, 78-79) with the meaning "to attack."

Lēctiō grammatica (87-127)

Students have now learned the complete first three declensions of nouns. Memorizing the paradigms should be easy, since the forms by now are all familiar. Special attention should be paid to third declension i-stem nouns, explained in *LATINE DISCO,* and to memorizing the gender of third declension nouns. All nouns have plural genitive in *-ium*, except: imparisyllabic nouns with only one consonant before the ending *–is* of singular genitive (ex.: *pastor –is; consul –is*: plural genitive: *-um*) There are a few other exceptions, which will be taught later on (ex: *canis –is*: gen. pl.: *canum*.)

Capitulum X: *BESTIAE ET HOMINES dēclīnātiō tertia; īnfinītīvus praes.*

Lēctiō prīma (1-34)

Active infinitives are introduced as complements to the forms *potest/possunt*. It is important that students understand that the enclitic *enim* (line 32), as the marginal note shows, always comes in second position—it is postpositive. Otherwise its meaning is identical to *nam*.

Lēctiō secunda (35-73)

In this *lēctiō* passive infinitives are presented. Students should note the forms *marium* in line 44 and *marī* in line 56; the complete declension of the irregular third-declension nouns *mare* and *animal* will be given at the end of the next chapter. Contrast *ovis* with *ōva* in line 71. Students should contrast the verb *parere* which gives the forms *parit* and *pariunt* in lines 72-73 with the verb *pārēre* encountered at IV 110.

Lēctiō tertia (74-131)

In line 77 *cane* is feminine since the dog in question is a bitch. Dogs are generically masculine, however, and so the general statement in line 84 renders *canis* as masculine.

Students will readily understand the accusative + infinitive construction with verbs of perception (lines 80, 83, 113, 114, 120, 121, 126, 131), but these examples should be closely examined since they are preparing the way for a more comprehensive study of the object clauses in the next *capitulum*. 112 is *ablātīvus modī* (*cf. 9.90*), usually expressed with *cum*, but not always as here w. accompanying adjective

Lēctiō grammatica (132-183)

The infinitives of all verbs encountered up to now are presented here; the instructor should make sure that students have memorized all infinitive forms so as to recognize to which of the four conjugations each verb belongs. Special care should be taken with pronunciation: infinitives of second conjugation verbs are always accented on the second-to-last syllable (the penult), those of third conjugation verbs on the third-to-last syllable (antepenult). Failure to observe the stress accent will result in confusion between the two conjugations. Likewise, the instructor should ensure that students memorize the third declension noun paradigms here given together with the gender of the new third declension nouns.

Capitulum XI: CORPUS HUMANUM *accūsātīvus cum īnfīnītīvō; dēclīnātiō tertia (neutr.) prōnōmina possessīva*

Lēctiō prīma (1-41)

In bracchiō and *in crūre* (line 3) are equivalent to *in extrēmō bracchiō* and *in extrēmō crūre*.

In line 7, as often, the second element of the comparison is suppressed (elision): *capillus* is understood after *quam*. The expressions *bene audīre/male audīre* presented here (15-16) with their literal meaning, also mean idiomatically "to have a good/bad reputation." This sense derives from the expression "*audīre bene/ male (loquī dē sē) ab aliquō*" as in Greek "*kalōs/kakōs akouein*." The literal sense of this expression is often presented, to avoid ambiguity, by the expressions *distīnctē, liquidē, clārē audīre* or conversely *parum, graviter audīre*. The double sense also gave rise to word play, as in Cicero: *Erat surdāster M. Crassus, sed aliud molestius, quod male audiēbat!* (*Tusc. 5.116*)—"Marcus Crassus was deaf, but what's worse, he had a bad reputation!"

Lēctiō secunda (42-91)

The construction with *iubēre* is introduced here together with that of other verbs that govern the accusative and infinitive construction. Only later will *iubēre* be introduced with the passive infinitive, while the personal construction will be found in the second volume. Students might be encouraged to reflect that *Iūlius servum suum Tūsculum īre iubet* can be rendered in English as "Julius orders that his slave go to Tusculum," or as "Julius orders his slave to go to Tusculum."

Line 55 is the first appearance of the *ablātīvus causae*.

Lēctiō tertia (92-139)

Here the two different constructions with *verba affectuum* are juxtaposed in lines 114 and 118: *Aemilia gaudet quod fīlius vīvit* and *Syra Quīntum vīvere gaudet*.

Lēctiō grammatica (140-179)

A convenient list of third declension nouns according to gender is here presented; students should memorize the genders of all third declension nouns encountered heretofore. For the neuter two different declension are here presented: that of *corpus* or *flūmen*, and several other listed neuter nouns, and the declension of *mare* or *animal*. All neuter nouns ending in –*e*, -*al*, and –*ar* follow this same declension.

168-179 presents an important review of accusative/ infinitive constructions encountered up to now.

Capitulum XII: MILES ROMANUS *datīvus possessīvus 6-10; prōnōmina possessīva 25, resumed in 14.64, 77, 86, adiectīvum (dēcl. I/II), comparātīvus 199-225; datīvus + pārēre etc. dēclīnātiō tertia (adiectīvum), dēclīnātiō quārta; genetīvus partītīvus; genetīvus quālitātis*

Lēctiō prīma (1-35)

The *dativus possessōris* introduced here with *nomen* (9) can be an occasion for students to give their own names: *Mihi nōmen est...* Students might be interested to learn that *Eī nomen est 'Lūcius Iūlius Balbus'* can also be rendered *Eī nōmen est 'Lūcio Iūlio Balbō,'* putting the proper name in agreement with the dative *eī*.

The list of *praenōmina* and their abbreviations given in the margin next to line 14 ff. is well worth memorizing, since these forms appear frequently in Latin literature.

The students should be led to compare *pīlum* (34) and its plural *pīla* with the noun *pila* met at X 74.

Lēctiō secunda (36-91)

The construction indicating extent, e.g. *sex pedēs* (47) is the *accūsātīvus spatiī* (=accusative of extent of space).

Note the several elisions of *gladius* (53-59). Already in the preceding chapter we have seen the omission of the demonstrative with the second term of the comparison (with a comparison of equivalence). Here the same omission appears with a comparison of greater size (called, as in the ancient grammars, simply *comparātīvus*). The phrase *Gladius equitis longior et gravior est quam peditis* contrasts with the following *Gladius eius...est... brevior et levior quam is quī ab equite fertur* and also with *Etiam gladiī quī ā Germānīs feruntur longiōrēs et graviōrēs sunt quam*

Rōmānōrum.

The construction of *imperāre* with the dative (82) should be contrasted with that of *iubēre +acc./infin.* given in the previous *capitulum.* The teacher can devise substitution drills, replacing one construction with the other.

Lēctiō tertia (92-142)

Capitulum XIII: ANNUS ET MENSES adiectīvum (dēcl. III), superlātīvus (-issimus) 167-176, comparātiō adiectīvī 168-176; numerī ōrdinālēs 2-6, 54

Lēctiō prīma (1-45)

Students should be understand that, although *centum* is indeclinable, *ducentī* and *trecentī* (7-11) decline like other first and second declension adjectives.

19, 44, 46, 52 *ablātīvus temporis*

Lēctiō secunda (46-101)

Lūna 'nova' esse dīcitur: The instructor should point out the use of the nominative with verbs like *dīcī.*

To remember the months with the nones on the seventh and the ides on the fifteenth the mnemonic formula "Marmaijuloct" may be helpful (66-67), or the formula given in Gildersleeve's *Latin Grammar:*

> In March, July, October, May,
> The Ides are on the fifteenth day,
> The Nones the seventh, but all besides,
> Have two days less for Nones and Ides.

The genders of the seasons must be memorized: *aestās* (f.), *hiems* (f.), *vēr* (n.), *autumnus* (m.)

The different meanings of *petere* are recalled in line 100.

Lēctiō tertia (102-149)

The expression *tempus est dormīre* is close in meaning to *necesse est dormīre.*

Capitulum XIV: NOVUS DIES prōnōmina interrogātīva uter 12, adiectīvum (comparātiō), participium praes. 134-150,

Lēctiō prīma (1-32)

(11) Students should understand that in expressions such as *alter ē duōbus* the prepositions *ē, ex* with the ablative have a partitive value: "out of two, of the two." Such constructions will appear with some frequency from now on.

Fenestrā apertā (15) and *fenestrā clausā* (18) are the first two examples of the ablative absolute, which will be more fully introduced in *capitulum XVI*; there is no need to explain the construction now, as long as students understand its circumstantial force. The teacher may ask students to paraphrase *Puer gallum canentem audit.* They might respond *Puer audit gallum qui canit* or *Puer audit gallum canere.* If *audīvī Iūlium loquentem dē mē* means "I heard Julius (while he was) talking about me, *audīvī Iūlium loquī dē mē* can express two slightly different concepts: (1) "I heard Julius was talking about me," (direct perception) and (2) "I heard that Julius was speaking about me" (indirect information). One of many examples which can be understood in the first way is the verse of Plautus (*Epid.* 246): *Egomet, postquam id illās*

audīvī loquī… "I, having heard that they were saying this…" The same applies with *vidēre: video eum hoc facientem* means "I see him while he is doing this," while *video eum hoc facere* can mean either "I see him doing this" (e.g. Caesar, *B.G.* 2.34.3: *Hūc tōta Vārī conversa aciēs suōs fugere et concīdī vidēbat*) or "I see/ notice that he did this." This difference between the construction of *verba sentiendī* with the accusative and infinitive and that with the participle is not always strongly felt in Latin authors.

Lēctiō secunda (33-74)

In this first volume of the course *poscere* is presented with the most frequent classical construction, that with *ā/ab* and the ablative: *Mārcus vestīmenta sua ā servō poscit.* In line 102 we find: *Mārcus autem magnum mālum ā patre poscit.* When we meet the verb *docēre* in chapter XVII the less usual construction of *poscere* with the double accusative may be mentioned.

Lēctiō tertia (75-132)

In line 78 we meet for the first time the construction of *praeter* with the accusative.

(87) Students should understand that the forms *mēcum, sēcum,* and, in line 108 (repeated in line 117) *tēcum* are composed of the preposition *cum* postpositive (coming after) the personal pronoun.

(104) Students should here memorize the imperative of *esse,* and recognize that the long *ē* distinguishes it from the imperative of *esse.*

(115) Point out the very important adjective *omnis, -e.*

Capitulum XV: MAGISTER ET DISCIPULI esse (ind. praes.) 143-153; īre (ind. praes.) 166-167; locātīvus 81; persōnae 130-139; persōnae verbī (āct.) 130-170; prōnōmina persōnālia ego, tū, nōs, vōs (nom.) 132-133, posse (ind. praes.) 169-170

Lēctiō prīma (1-40)

(2) Students who already understand the word *lūdere* may find it difficult to conceive of school as a "game." A similar sense lies behind the Greek word *scholē,* English "school." The following passage from *Ludovicus Vives* is pertinent:

> *Lusius: Nōn ludimus hodiē?*
> *Aeschines: Nōn, nam dies est operarius. Eho, tu venisse tē hūc arbitrāris lusum? Nōn est hīc lūdendī locus, sed studendī.*
> *Lus.: Cūr ergo ludus nōminātur?*
> *Aesch.: Nominatur quidem lūdus, sed litterārius; quia litterīs est hīc ludendum, alibi pīlā, trochō, talīs; et Graecē audīvī appellārī scholam, quasī otium, quod vērum sit otium, et animī quies aetātem in studiīs agere."* (*Exercit. Ling. Latin., cap. V: Lectio*).

(16-18) The difference between the static sense of *sedēre* and that, implying movement, of *(cōn-)sīdere* is apparent from the example. The schoolmaster orders: *"cōnsīde!"* Sextus sits down: *Sextus in sellā cōnsīdit.* Finally Sextus stays seated in his chair: *Discipulus tacitus ante magistrum sedet.* This alternation of sense is found in many other compounds, e.g. *assidēre/assīdere; īnsidēre/īnsīdere; obsidēre/obsīdere; possidēre/possīdere,* etc.

(23) Unless students raise the question, one may omit mention of the accusative of exclamation, the *accūsatīvus*

exclamātīvus, that will be treated explicitly in chapter XXIX. If it is discussed in class it should be contrasted with '*Ō improbī discipulī!*' in lines 101-102.

Lēctiō secunda (41-95)

(81) This first encounter with the locative *domī* will be followed by an explicit discussion the *Student's manual* on chapter XX. The function of the locative may be mentioned at this point, recalling the form *Tūsculī* which students have already encountered.

Lēctiō tertia (96-128)

(97) *Prior*, indicating the first of two, can be contrasted with *prīmus*, the first of many. *Prior* is actually a comparative, while *prīmus* is a superlative.

Capitulum XVI: TEMPESTAS ablātīvus absolūtus; verbum dēpōnēns (152-165)

Lēctiō prīma (1-40)

(1) *Quōrum* is the first example of a partitive genitive drawn from the pronoun; it is explained in the margin as the equivalent of *ex quibus*.

(7) The sense of *ad* here = *apud* should be mentioned.

Lēctiō secunda (41-95)

(34) This construction of *aquā* in the *ablātīvus abundantiae* (really a variety of the *ablātīvus īnstrūmentī*) may give occasion for the teacher to recall the possible use of *plēnus* with the ablative as well as the genitive. See on VII (43) above.

(45-49) These lines present the opportunity for a repetition and clarification of the construction with double nominatives of verbs such as *dīci, appellari*, etc.

(50-51) The dative of reference may be here explained with other examples.

Lēctiō tertia (96-150)

Capitulum XVII: NUMERI DIFFICILES persōnae verbī (pass.) 154-162, praesens ind. 154-193, adverbium –ō 12; verbum dēpōnēns (187-193), numerī 19-35

Lēctiō prīma (1-41)

(1-3) Students should note and commit to memory that *docēre* governs the double accusative. This construction is comparable to the English: *Magister puerōs numerōs et litterās docet = The teacher teaches the boys numbers and letters*.

(29) In expressions such as *longum est* Latin uses the indicative where English would use the conditional.

Lēctiō secunda (42-87)

(60-61) *Cōgitāre nōn potes!* = *You can't think!* In this expression the verb *posse* has the sense, already indicated in chapter XI, of "to be capable of something."

(79-80) *Amīcus* and *inimīcus* have up to now been encountered as substantives with the genitive, e.g. VI, 44-45: *Dāvus amīcus Mēdī nōn est... Mēdus est inimīcus Dāvī. Ursus autem amīcus Dāvī est*. Here we find them as adjectives construed with the dative: *Magister amīcus est patribus vestrīs, patrī meō inimīcus*. From this distinction derives the difference between the possessive adjective (comparable to a genitive) and the dative of the personal pronoun: cf. Cic., *Att. Ille noster amīcus, vir optimus et mihi amīcissimus*. To help students understand the difference between the substantival and the adjective senses of *amīcus* and *inimīcus*, contrast the English phrases *Titus is my friend* (substantive) and *Titus is friendly to me* (adjective.)

(81) With *quamquam* we begin to encounter concessive constructions. It may be that its sense will not be immediately obvious to students. Lead them to reflect on the overall sense of the passage to determine its meaning. Various English translations are possible: *even if, although, notwithstanding that...*

Lēctiō tertia (88-152)

(94-95) Marcus's response is an occasion to point out that, while rhetorical questions may expect a certain response, there is no guarantee that the addressee will provide the expected response. Here the teacher is confident of inspiring fear with his switch, but Marcus, impertinent as usual, contradicts his expectations and denies that he is afraid.

(110-111) Here *oportet* is presented in its infinitival construction.

Capitulum XVIII: LITTERAE LATINAE superlātīvus (-errimus, -illimus) 73, 84, 102, adverbium (-ē,-iter 194-212), comparātiō adverbiī 206-212; numerī adv. Semel... -iēs 118-126, 134, superlātīvus adverbiī 206-212

Lēctiō prīma (1-61)

(41) Here *quisque* is introduced. The declension is obviously identical to that of *quis, quae, quod* with the indeclinable enclitic *–que* added as a suffix.

(58) In the phrase *Sextus ūnus ex tribus puerīs rēctē scrībit* the sense of *ūnus = alone, only* should be emphasized. *Out of the three boys, only Sextus/Sextus alone writes correctly.*

Lēctiō secunda (62-118)

(65) Students may think of the sense of the Latin word *quālis* in relation to the English derivative *quality*.

(67) Here we find an example of *suus* referring to the logical subject of the clause: *Magister suam cuique discipulō tabulam reddit*. We recommend that students linger over this construction, and memorize examples of this type: *suus*, and never *eius*, is used with *quisque*.

(97) *Nōn semper idem dīcimus atque scrībimus* will probably be understood by students in the sense of: *we don't always say and write the same thing*. This is in fact the original and correct sense of the phrase. Thus, for example, in Cicero *Dē off. 1.30: Aliter dē illīs ac dē nōbis iūdicāmus* can be understood, giving *ac* its fundamental copulative sense, *we judge about them and about us in a different manner*. This copulative sense gives way to a comparative one in the mind of the speaker. It may be pointed out that *atque* has this value after adjectives or adverbs such as *similis, īdem, alius, contrā, perinde*, etc., as Priscian points out: *Frequenter Latīnī ac et atque in sīgnificātiōne similitūdinis accipiunt*. The Jesuit precept comes to mind, commanding obedience *perinde ac cadāver*.

Lēctiō tertia (119-192)

(122) In the phrase *Mārcus, ut piger discipulus, quater tantum V scrībit...* the *ut* develops a causal nuance (= because he is, lazy student that he is) out of its fundamental comparative value = like, as.

(145) To understand the phrase *Mārcus stilum vertit et litteram H dēlet* it may help students to learn what a *stilus* was like: on one end it was pointed, to incise letters on the wax tablet; on the other end it was flat so as to flatten the wax and rub out what was previously incised. *Verte stilum!* meant to turn over the *stilus* so as to erase (*ērādere, dēlēre*) the letters.

(163) The use of *ex* + abl. to express the material of which something is composed is here a new construction. In chapter XXII the same construction with adjectives such as *ferreus, aureus*, etc. will be introduced, so it is not necessary to dwell on it here.

(183) It may be pointed out that the expression *quōque mēnse = singulīs mēnsibus*. Students may be asked the meaning of *tertiō quōque mēnse*. Such expressions will be developed in chapter XX. Vowel quantity is essential in distinguishing *quōque* from *quoque*.

(190) In the expression *ad diem* the preposition indicates coincidence with a point in time. Cf. Cicero, *Tūsc.* 5.22: *admonuit ut pecūniam ad diem solverent;* also, Cic. *Att.* 16.16A: *nostra ad diem dictam fīent.*

Capitulum XIX: MARITUS ET UXOR praesens/praeteritum (imperf.) 155-162; esse (imperf.) 168-184; genitīvus quālitātis 19.33; imperfectum ind. 164-208

Lēctiō prīma (1-58)

(3-4) Students were introduced to the ablative of instrument already in chapter VIII, but they may still be struck by the construction *Tēctum peristylī altīs columnīs sustinētur...*It may be worth pointing out that the instrumental ablative designates an efficient cause which is not a personal agent; the ablative of personal agent construction would of course require the preposition *ā* or *ab*.

(15-21) This is a suitable *locus* for elaborating partitive constructions. The partitive can be expressed with the genitive, *ē* or *ex* with the ablative, or with *inter* + accusative as here: *Inter omnēs deōs deāsque Iuppiter pessimus marītus est.* The superlative can also be followed by a partitive genitive, as in line 21, although this partitive genitive need not be explicit: e.g. *In hāc bibliothēcā centum librī sunt: pulcherrimus est ille quī 'Dē officiīs' īnscrībitur.*

(33) Here two constructions indicating age are treated: 1) *Mārcus octō annōs habet*—a classical construction, found in Cicero, Livy, Nepos, and others, and 2) *Quīntus est puer septem annōrum* with the genitive of quality, perhaps a more frequent construction.

Lēctiō secunda (59-88)

(83) It may be pointed out that in a phrase like *post ūnum annum* the word *post* functions as a preposition and thus governs the accusative, while the same word serves as an adverb in a construction like *annō post*, where *annō* serves as an ablative of time when or within which. The construction encountered in line

38 *ante decem annōs* may be contrasted with *decem annīs post* in line 86.

Lēctiō tertia (89-153)

(90-96) This chapter provides several examples of the characteristic intransitive constructions with passive verbs, e.g. *amor meus tempore nōn minuitur* (90-91) and *Tempus amōrem meum nōn minuit, immō vērō auget!* (95-96)

(110) Here the construction of *dīgnus* with the ablative is introduced. Constructions of *dīgnus* with *quī, quae, quod* and the subjunctive will be introduced later.

(133) The phrase *Num hodiē minus pulchra sum quam tunc eram?* illustrates the comparative with *minus...quam*.

(149) Here is the first appearance of *opus est*. At line 152 it will be encountered with the infinitive: *Num opus est mē plūs dīcere?*

Capitulum XX: PARENTES futūrum (167-207); esse (fut.) 176-188

Lēctiō prīma (1-46)

(2) It should be noted that *cūnae, -ārum* is a *plūrāle tantum*—a word that normally occurs only in the plural number.

(6) Students should understand that *carēre* governs the ablative of privation (a form of the ablative of separation), as *implēre* has already been seen to govern the ablative of abundance.

(10-11) Note the ablatives of means *pāne* and *lacte* in the phrase *parvulus infāns...nōn pāne, sed lacte vīvit*.

(39) Here is a first example of the disjunctive direct interrogative construction in *–ne...an: māterne, an nūtrīx?* The construction with *utrum...an* will be met in chapter XXVIII.

Lēctiō secunda (47-102)

(84-96) It may be noted that in a phrase such as *hoc est mātris officium* the word *officium* could easily be suppressed, in which case we could speak of a "genitive of pertinence" (= it is characteristic of, it is the duty of...) Likewise the phrase *meum officium est...*the word *officium* could be omitted: *meum est pecūniam facere = my duty, my task is to make money*.

Lēctiō tertia (103-164)

(104) Students should note that *occurrere* governs the dative.

(120) *Sīve* was first encountered alone at XVI.2 and, with a slight difference of sense, in line 12 of this chapter. Here it is presented in coordination with another *sīve: sīve mare tranquillum sīve turbidum est*. Note that Latin uses the indicative mood in such expressions with disjunctive particles,

(123-124) Here is the accusative of exclamation, which will be explained in chapter XXIX of *LATINE DISCO*.

(135) This is an opportunity to review the discussion of constructions such as *tertiō quōque diē* in the notes on chapter XVIII.

(158-159) Here is the relative impersonal construction *mē decet*.

***Capitulum XXI: PUGNA DISCIPULORUM** imperfectum ind./ perfectum 152-158 dēclīnātiō quārta (neutr.); īnfīnītīvus perf. 166, 175-6, 202; locātīvus 20, participium perf. (pass.) 193-196, perfectum ind. 159-206; perfectum īnf. 166, 175-6, 202; perfectum/imperfectum 152-158*

Lēctiō prīma (1-26)

(20) Note here the locative *humī*, which will be repeated several times (50-51, 74). Students will recall *domī*, while *rūrī* will be encountered at XXVII 66.

Lēctiō secunda (27-78)

(28) Students may here linger over the expression *cum prīmum* meaning *as soon as*. Comparable constructions such as *simul ac/atque* and *ubi prīmum* will be encountered in chapters XXX and XXXII.

(30) Note the irregular vocative forms of *meus* and *fīlius*: *mī fīlī!*

(64) There is a significant difference in vowel quantity between *solum* and *sōlum*.

Lēctiō tertia (79-149)

(79) *Postquam* with the perfect indicative here indicates immediate succession.

***Capitulum XXII: CAVE CANEM** ferre (ind. praes.) 105-111; genitīvus quālitātis 16*

Lēctiō prīma (1-55)

(1) *Cōnstāre* together with *ē/ex* and the ablative meaning *to be made of, consist of* is here presented for the first time. Lines 13-21 will provide examples with the ablative of material: *catēna ex ferrō/catēna cōnstat ē multīs ānulīs ferreīs.*

(16) The phrase *Aurum est māgnī pretiī sīcut gemmae* gives an opportunity to review the genitive of quality. Normally the distinction is made between moral (that is to say, non-physical) qualities expressed in the genitive or the ablative, and physical qualities expressed with the ablative. The genitive expresses spatial-temporal descriptions and descriptions relative to quantity and value. It expresses the quality as a category to which the person or thing belongs, or one that defines the person or thing. By contrast with the characterizing force of the genitive, the function of the ablative is instrumental or sociative—it indicates the quality as something that accompanies but does not define the individual or the object. In the case of this passage the "great value" is a quality by which the speaker characterizes gold; it is an essential quality of gold, and not merely an accompaniment. We emphasize the point of view of the speaker, since this value could in another example express a purely subjective valuation of a defining characteristic. E.g., one might speak of a *mnēmosynum māgnī pretiī*—a memory of great value, though it might have no objective value. This is why even physical qualities, when they are exceptionally represented as essential characteristics, may be also be represented in the genitive case, as when Caesar mentions (B.G. 2.30.4) that the Gauls deprecated the Romans as *hominēs tantulae statūrae*—evidently the Gauls here regard their short stature as a defining characteristic of the Romans.

(23) From this point on students will encounter ablative absolutes ever more frequently, whether with present or past perfect participles. Compare the examples at line 30 and at line 119 of this chapter; the latter example was anticipated at XXI 96: *magistrō recitante*. To elaborate the discussion in *LATINE DISCO* one might observe that 1) in an ablative absolute there should be no grammatical link with the subject of the main verb of the sentences (there should be no pronoun referring to the main subject) and 2) the present participle can form an ablative absolute for all verbs, while the past participle can form an ablative absolute only with deponent verbs that are intransitive and with verbs that are transitive in the active voice.

(29) *Quīn* may be explained to students as deriving from *quī* (an archaic ablative of *quī. quae, quod* meaning *how?*) + the negation *ne = nōn.* Thus the literal sense of the word is *how not? = why not?* It is used in the interrogative to indicate an invitation or a polite command. It may suffice to tell students, as the marginal note indicates, that *quīn* is equivalent to *cūr nōn…?* or to an imperative (*Cūr nōn aperīs? Aperī!*). Other uses of *quīn* will be studied in *ROMA AETERNA* beginning with chapter XL.

(38) In classical authors, and particularly comic writers, the formula *quid est tibi nōmen?* is more frequent than the more regular form *quod est tibi nōmen?* E.g. Plautus, *Amph.* 1.364: *Quid ais? Quid nōmen tibi est?*; *Men.* 3.498: *Respondē, adulēscēns, quaesō, quid nōmen tibist?*; *Pers.* 4. 623: *Quid nōmen tibist?*; *Pseud.* 2.744: *Quid nōmen esse dīcam istī servō?*; *Rud.* 4.1160: *In ēnsiculo quid nōmen est paternum?*; *Trin.* 4.889: *quid est tibi nōmen, adulēscēns?*

(43) The phrase *nōmen meum nōn est facile dictū: Tlēpolemus nōminor* not only introduces the passive supine in *-ū* but also gives an opportunity to repeat the alternative dative of possession construction: *Mihi nōmen est… (Tlēpolemus/ Tlēpolemō)* and to reinforce that appellative verbs take a double nominative construction. In this case one of the nominatives is implicit: *(ego) Tlēpolemus nōminor.*

Lēctiō secunda (56-121)

(56) Take care that students do not confuse the adverb *forīs* with the feminine noun *foris, -is.* Further on (lines 115, 117, 118) *forās* will be encountered. *Forīs* indicates place where, *forās* motion towards. Both forms derive from *fora*, a doublet of *foris* that does not otherwise appear. Ernout-Meillet (*Dictionnaire étymologique de la langue latine,* Klincksieck, Paris, 1994, s.v. *forēs*) comments that the notion "outside" is often expressed by forms meaning "at the door." With these Latin constructions one may compare Armenian *durs* (locative and accusative), Greek *thyraze (thyras-de*)* and *thyrda: exo.*

(60-65) Already the illustration at the beginning of the chapter, taken from the famous mosaic at the house of the tragic poet at Pompei, will have conveyed to students that *cave canem* means *beware of the dog!* This meaning is here explained. It may be opportune to explain to students that *cavēre* means "to be attentive" and that, construed with the accusative or with *ā/ab* + abl. it means to avoid doing something, while with the dative it means to pay attention to something.

(67) The teacher may draw the students's attention to *propius*, the comparative degree of *prope.*

(77) Note that *sinere* has the same construction as *iubēre*; other examples will appear at lines 86 and 114.

(84) It may be explained that with the advective *tōtus* the place where can be expressed by the ablative preceded by *in* or by the ablative alone. The difference consists in the fact that the ablative with *in* is applied to a static verbal process which fixes one or more points within a space (e.g. Cic. *Phil.* 10.10: *Tria tenet oppida tōtō in orbe terrārum*—the whole surface of the earth is not referred to, but rather several points on the earth) whereas the ablative without a preposition is construed with a dynamic verbal process, the movement of which extends over the whole space in question: (e.g. Cic. *Dē nāt. deōr.* 2.95: *tōtō caelō lūce diffūsā*). This line depicts a dynamic verbal action which is not localized in one or more points in the space in question, but rather extends to the whole surface of the body. The construction of the ablative without a preposition can also be interpreted as a type of ablative of means, comparable to the ablative of route with nouns of passage such as *viā, portā, ponte,* etc.

(92) It may be explained that *amābō tē* is a polite expression, comparable to *ōrō tē* = *please, I beg you.*

Capitulum XXIII: EPISTULA MAGISTRI *futūrum part. & īnf. 157-178; participium fut. 157-165*

Lēctiō prīma (1-40)

(2) Students should recognize that the quantity of the vowel -*ē*- distinguishes the present from the perfect tense in the verb *venīre* and its compounds.

(4-11) Here two more local adverbs are introduced: *illinc* and *hinc*. It may be pointed out that -*n*- is characteristic of adverbs of motion from a place: *unde, hinc, illinc*. Students will encounter *inde* in chapter XXIX.

(26) *Neque umquam* is glossed in the margin here as simply = *et numquam*. A more ample discussion will be found in *LATINE DISCO,* chapter XXVI.

(28) Students should note that in phrases such as this one *nēmō* has the value of an adjective comparable to *nūllus*. It is as though one were saying, *nēmō, quī sit magister*. The sense is thus pronominal also here.

(36) *Ob* and *propter* with the accusative express a causal complement, representing a cause external to the subject.

Lēctiō secunda (41-83)

(57) This is yet another example of where Latin uses the indicative where we might expect a conditional or subjunctive: *Mārcus prope omnia fēcit quae facere nōn dēbuit.*

(79) Impersonal verbal constructions are now being introduced; *pudet* alone needs to be learned here, but the teacher may wish to point out that *piget, paenitet,* etc. take the same construction. There are other examples in this chapter at lines 82-83, 138-139. The old explanation of the Port-Royal grammar may be helpful: *mē pudet factī* = *pudor factī mē tenet* = *the shame of the deed holds me*. Compare Horace, *Epist.* 1.18.24: *quem paupertātis pudor... tenet*. The same equivalence exists with other verbs: *mē taedet huius reī* = *taedium huius reī mē tenet; mē paenitet huius reī* = *paenitentia huius reī mē tenet; mē miseret illīus hominis* = *misericordia illīus hominis mē tenet; mē huius reī piget* = *pigritia huius reī mē tenet;* cf. Sen. *Dē tranq. an.* 2.8: *illōs paenitentia coeptī tenet.*

Lēctiō tertia (84-155)

Capitulum XXIV: PUER AEGROTUS *ablātīvus comparātiōnis, verbum dēpōnēns ind./īnf. perf. 30, 77, 90, 108, 116; plūsquamperfectum ind. 120-161*

Lēctiō prīma (1-51)

(18) *Mēne dormīre?* is an interrogative-exclamatory use of the infinitive. The subject is in the accusative, perhaps by analogy with the accusative of exclamation.

(33) Another example of the Latin indicative where we might expect a conditional: *facile os frangere potuistī*. Note the difference in vowel quantity between *os* and *ōs, ōris*. The later form *ossum* may have developed in connection with the loss of vowel quantity in the spoken language. Augustine uses both forms in his *Ēnārrātiōnēs in Psalmōs* in commenting on psalm 138, where *ossum* is understood to be the popular form and *os* the more noble usage: *Os suum dīcit: quod vulgō dīcitur ossum, Latīnē os dīcitur. Hoc in Graecō invenitur [ostoun]. Nam possēmus hīc putāre ōs esse, ab eō quod sunt ōra; nōn os correptē, ab eō quod sunt ossa. Nōn est ergō absconditum, inquit, os meum ā tē, quod fēcistī in absconditō. Habeō in absconditō quoddam ossum. Sīc enim potius loquāmur: melius est reprehendant nōs grammaticī, quam nōn intelligant populī. Ergō est, inquit, quoddam ossum meum intus in absconditō; tū fēcistī intus ossum mihi in absconditō, et nōn est absconditum ā tē. In absconditō enim fēcistī; sed numquid et tibi hoc abscondistī? Hoc ossum meum factum ā tē in absconditō hominēs nōn vident, hominēs nōn nōvērunt; tu autem nōstī, quī fēcistī. Quod ergō 'os' dīcit, frātrēs? Quaerāmus illud; in absconditō est. Sed quia Chrīstiānī in nōmine Dominī Chrīstiānīs loquimur, modo invēnimus quod sit ossum huiusmodī. Fīrmitās quaedam est interior; quia in ossibus fīrmitās et fortitūdō intelligitur.*

(38) After *quamquam* now *etsī* is introduced, again with the indicative. It will be repeated at lines 47, 51, 75. Concessive constructions with the subjunctive, such as *quamvīs, licet,* etc. will be studied in *ROMA AETERNA.*

Lēctiō secunda (52-117)

(59) *Certē sciō* = *certum est mē scīre; certō sciō* (note that *certō* appears only in this construction) by contrast indicates a certainty in the object of knowledge. The former indicates *it is a fact that I know,* the latter that *I know for certain* = *I know, and have no doubts about it.*

(60) It should be noted that *nōvisse,* although a perfect infinitive, has a present meaning: *certō sciō eum aliquam fēminam nōvisse* = *I know for certain that he knows some woman*. Thus in line 94, *canis tē nōvit, ignōrat illum* = *the dog knows you, but does not know him*. This is a logical perfect, with the literal meaning "to have come to know," and therefore "to know." Students will soon encounter *ōdisse* and *meminisse,* which bear comparison with *nōvisse.*

Capitulum XXV: THESEUS ET MINOTAUR *verbum dēpōnēns (imp.)146-154; genetīvus/accūsātīvus 22, 46, 51, 77, 86, 88, 122, 125, 130; genetīvus + oblivīscī/meminisse 126; locātīvus 132*

Lēctiō prīma (1-41)

(40) Note the adverb of place *illūc;* in line 53 students will encounter *ibi* and in line 74 *hūc*. It may be pointed out that

adverbs of motion towards feature –*ū*- or –*ō*-, as in *hūc, illūc, quō…*? *Eō* will appear in chapter XXVIII.

Lēctiō secunda (42-88)

(62) Students should note that *coepī* is strictly speaking not the perfect of *incipere*, but a separate perfect with no present stem (the form *coepiō* is archaic, appearing only in the comic poets and a few other authors.)

(73) The second appearance of the *ablātīvus causae*, which first appeared in chapter 11. It will be repeated in the next two chapters (**26**.24, **27**.109).

(74) It should be pointed out that the frequency of the ablative absolute construction in Latin reflects the absence of a perfect active participle. In Latin only deponent verbs have a perfect participle with active meaning, and thus they can be used directly where other verbs might appear in an ablative absolute: *Hortātus mīlitēs, Caesar commīsit proelium.*

Lēctiō tertia (89-144)

(117) The expression *montēs aurī pollicērī* appears in Terence (*Phorm. 1.68*); it is equivalent to English "to promise the sun and the moon."

Capitulum XXVI: DAEDALUS ET ICARUS gerundium (147-162), imperātīvus futūrī 81

Lēctiō prīma (1-31)

At the end of this chapter it will be opportune to review all the different ways of expressing purpose encountered up to now: 1) with *causā/grātiā* + the preceding genitive of the gerund; 2) with *ad* + the accusative of the gerund; 3) with the supine in *–um* with verbs of motion. *Ut* with the subjunctive and the gerundive constructions will be presented in chapters XXVIII and XXXI. Other purpose constructions, such as relative clauses of purpose, will be presented in *ROMA AETERNA*.

(26) Here is *neque quisquam*, like *neque umquam* seen in chapter XXIII.

(27) The impersonal use of *iuvāre* will appear again in lines 32-33.

Lēctiō secunda (32-82)

(38) In the phrase *Quis est tam līber quam avis quae trāns mōntēs, vallēs, flūmina, maria, volāre potest?* students should be able to explain the significant vowel quantity in *līber* by contrast with *liber*.

(47) Students should pay special attention to the form *item*, the sense of which may not be immediately apparent.

(78) *Sīn*, like *quīn* in chapter XXII, represents the conjunction of *sī* + *ne* (=*nōn*). It can be used alone, or preceded by *sī*, in which case it introduces a second hypothesis contrary to the first one, as in Plautus *Merc. 3.589*: *sī domī sum, forīs est animus, sīn forīs sum, animus domīst…*

(80) *Ūrere* here presents another opportunity for reviewing the use of the passive voice with an intransitive meaning.

Lēctiō tertia (83-145)

(85) *Nisi* here introduces an exception, as often when it is preceded or followed by a negation (here by *neque quisquam fugam*

eōrum animadvertit.) From expressions like *nōn lēgērunt hunc librum nisi paucī hominēs = no one has read this book except for a few people = only a few people have read this book*. This readily leads to more or less equivalent constructions such as *nōn nisi paucī hominēs hunc librum lēgērunt*, where *nōn nisi* (sometimes written *nōnnisi*) has merely an adverbial force meaning "only" = *tantum, tantummodo, cf. nōn numquam/nōnnumquam = interdum, nōn nūllī/nōnnūllī = aliquī, etc.*

It should also be noted that *nisi* here does not serve as a hypothetical conjunction, and therefore it is followed by *aliquī* and not *quī*. The often-repeated rule that "after *sī, nisi, num,* and *nē, ali-* takes a holiday," is actually less than exact. In fact, *quis* and *quī* are not variants or secondary forms of *aliquis* and *aliquī* but altogether different words. *Aliquis* and *aliquī* indicate people whose existence is certain, even if their identity is unknown (*vēnit aliquis = someone came* [I don't know who, but someone certainly came]), whereas *quis* and *quī* allude to people whose very existence is hypothetical (*sī quis veniet = if someone will come*). It is true that after *sī, nisi, num* and *nē* the words *quis* and *quī* are used most frequently, but in fact neither *aliquis* nor *aliquī* are rare in this position. This reason for this is clear from what has just been said: these particles by their nature frequently introduce expressions with a hypothetical sense, but this is not always the case. Consider this example from Cicero, *Tusc. 4.72*: *Sī quis [amor] est in rērum nātūrā sine sollicitūdine, sine dēsīderiō, sine cūrā… Sīn autem est aliquis amor, ut est certē, quī nihil absit ab īnsāniā…* The first phrase represents a true hypothesis, but the second does not, as is apparent from the interjection *ut est certē*. Here are some more examples of *aliquis* in cases where the overly rigid school rule might seem to demand *quis*: Cic. *Tusc. 1.6*: *Sī aliquid ōrātōriae laudis nostrā attulimus industriā…*(here the hypothesis is purely rhetorical, owing to the tone of modesty with which Cicero wants to affirm that he has made important contributions to Roman oratory); Sen. *Dē vītā beātā 13.7: Quī voluptātem sequitur vidētur… perventūrus in turpia nisi aliquis distīnxerit illī voluptātes* (he who pursues pleasure will fall into base things, unless someone teaches him to distinguish, as the passage continues, between unrestrained and extravagant pleasures and those which are in accord with *nātūrāle dēsīderium*. Seneca here wants to energetically affirm the importance of a guide; it is not important who the guide be, what matters is that he exist.) Further on at 15.1 Seneca continues: "*Quid tamen*" inquit "*prohibet in ūnum virtūtem voluptātemque cōnfundī et ita efficī summum bonum ut idem et honestum et iūcundum sit?*" "*Quia pars honestī nōn potest esse nisi honestum, nec summum bonum habēbit sincēritātem suam sī aliquid in sē vīderit dissimile meliōrī*" (Here Seneca is refuting the Epicurean thesis which holds that the greatest good is both *honestum* and *iūcundum*, that is both virtue and pleasure. He comments that, were this the case, virtue would no longer maintain its *sincēritās*, its integrity or purety, because it would have in itself *aliquid* different from its best part, namely virtue. This *aliquid* is something real and determined, namely pleasure or *iūcundum*. Caesare writes (*B. G*, 7.20.6): *sī alicuius indiciō vocātī [intervēnerint]…* meaning, if the attack of the Romans is made possible by the revelations of a traitor—thus *aliquis* alludes to a real and not a hypothetical person. From the didactic point of view it might happen that a student who studied the introductory discussion of this subject at *LATINE DISCO* XXII, where the argument is presented in very elementary terms, might be perplexed by the use of *aliquī* in this passage. But in fact the note to chapter XXII does not say that *quis* and *quid* are always to be used after *sī* and *num*, but that when they are so used they serve not as interrogatives but as indefinite pronouns. The explanations above, simplified and adapted to the level of the students, may help the teacher address such difficulties should they arise. This is not to deny that the mnemonic formula "after *sī, nisi, num,* and *nē, ali-* takes a holiday" can be didactically useful, so long as students are aware of its empirical and non-scientific character.

(88) It is worth going over the name of cities in union with an appellative verb, even when, as here, accompanied by an attribute.

(93-97) It is important that students practice the construction with the verb *vidērī*, as explained in *LATINE DISCO*. (The teacher may devise exercises extemporaneously or prepare them in advance.) The dative with this construction is a dative *iūdicantis* reflecting a point of view. *Hoc mihi vidētur esse bonum* = *this seems good from my point of view* = *this seems good to me.*

(122) In chapter XIII students already encountered the expression *tempus est dormīre,* which was probably explained as equivalent to *necesse est dormīre.* In this passage students encounter *tempus est dormiendī.* It may be worthwhile to clarify that while *tempus est* + infinitive emphasizes the necessity of the action by emphasizing the verb, the gerund underlines that it is time, the right moment, to sleep. In the former case *dormīre* is the determinate subject of *tempus est,* while in the latter *dormiendī* is the complement that specifies what *tempus* is at issue.

Capitulum XXVII: RES RUSTICAE *coniūnctīvus praes.* 182-235; *esse (coniūnctīvus praes.)* 195-209; *indicātīvus/coniūnctivus* 185-190, *locātīvus* 66

Lēctiō prīma (1-49)

(19) *Cōpia, -ae* is introduced here in the singular; the plural will appear in chapter XVI of *ROMA AETERNA.*

(29) (42) Note the expression *bis terve in annō* and supply comparable examples: *semel in annō, quater in mēnse,* etc.

Lēctiō secunda (50-114)

(55) It is clear that *nē... quidem* signifies "not even" from the context and the marginal note. It should be pointed out that the negated word always appears between *nē* and *quidem*

(65) Although the *negōtia* about which Julius is thinking are not political duties but private business, this passage presents an opportunity to talk about *ōtium* and *negōtium* in the Roman world. The phrase *in ōtiō cōgitat dē negōtiīs* is actually extrapolated from a context (*Dē off.,* 3.1) where Cicero compares his forced inactivity with the voluntary retirement from civil services of Scipio Africanus. Cicero's attitude shows how, for a Roman of the republic, solitude and meditation acquired value as preparation for a greater engagement in political and social life. It was held that private life lacked true nobility and dignity if it made no contribution to the *rēs pūblica.*

(66) After having learned *domī* and *humī* students now encounter *rūrī,* which should be easily comprehensible by analogy with the other two. Students should memorize this form, and recall that this noun is neuter, and that the accusative of motion towards will therefore be *rūs.*

(76) Students should understand that *quīdam,* met here

for the first time, has the same declension as *quī, quae, quod,* with the indeclinable *–dam* as a suffix.

(83) Students should recognize that the cause of an impediment is expressed by *prae* + ablative, and recall that an exterior cause by contrast is expressed by *ob* or *propter* + accusative.

(89) An expression of the type *iam trēs mēnsēs* implies that the duration continues, that is to say that Julius is still waiting. If the deed were completed (if, for example, Julius had said "three months ago I got the money") *abhinc* + acc. or the abl. would have been used. Another example of this construction will be found in line 120.

(94) *Tantum pecūniae* is an expression with a partitive genitive on the model of many others already encountered (e.g. *multum aquae, paulum cibī,* etc.) and thus should present no problem. Students should take care not to confuse *tantum, -ī* with the adverb *tantum* = *only.*

(94-95) Here is shown how to say "within how much time" a given thing will happen or should happen (*intrā* + acc.) Other examples appear in lines 113-114.

(108) The teacher might point out this use of *per* in prayers, adjurations, oaths, and exclamations.

Lēctiō tertia (115-180)

(30) Students should memorize that *prōdesse* governs the dative.

(138) Here is another example of the accusative of exclamation; a fuller treatment of the subject will be given in chapter XXIX.

(151) It is important that students commit to memory that *nēquam* is indeclinable.

(169-175) As the marginal note suggests, is should be explained that *prohibēre* comes from *prō* + *habēre* = *to hold in front* = *at a distance.* The long vowel of the prefix is shortened before the vowel *a,* since the aspirate *h* does not prevent application of the rule *vōcālis ante vōcālem corripitur.* From this etymological explanation the sense of the construction with *ā/ab* and the ablative will be clear: *prohibē ovēs tuās ab agrīs; nōlī mē officiō meō prohibēre.* A little further on the infinitival construction will be found: *Ego tē nōn prohibēbō officium facere. Prohibēre* often has the same construction as *iubēre, sinere,* etc.

(177) *Quam celerrimē potest* is glossed in the marginal note as *tam celeriter quam māximē fierī potest.* It may be explained that *quam* reinforces the superlative, and that the verb *posse* is not always expressed. *Hoc faciam quam celerrimē poterō* may be rendered more simply as *hoc faciam quam celerrimē; quam brevissimē fierī potest* or *quam brevissimē.*

Capitulum XXVIII: PERICULA MARIS *coniūnctīvus imperf.* 191-232; *esse (coniūnctīvus imperf.)* 201-213

This chapter presents a first encounter with original texts. A selection of passages from the *Vestus Latina* text of Matthew is inserted into the narrative. At this point it will become apparent that, not only do the original texts present no special difficulties of understanding, but that students will find them even easier than the composed Latin to which they have gradually become accustomed.

Lēctiō prīma (1-55)

(8-9) The correlation of *ut... ita* may be remarked.

(12) Notably: 1) *Quid...?* is here used in the sense of *cūr...?*, a frequent usage in classical authors: e.g. Cic., *Phil.*, 2.38.99: *ēloquere, quid vēnistī?* and *Prō Mil.*, 16.44: *Sed quid ego argūmentor, quid plūra disputō?* 2) The direct disjunctives *utrum... an...?* are here introduced. Another example will appear in line 20.

(100)   Here is the adverb *eō:* it should be commented that the vowels characteristic of motion from constructions are *–ō* or *–ū-*: *quō, eō, hūc, illūc.*

(37) This *locus* is an opportunity to underline the difference between *omnis, ūniversus* and *tōtus: omnis* designates a whole analyzed into its parts; *tōtus* synthetically designates a whole as a compact and undifferentiated unity; while *ūniversus* indicates the whole as a complex by contrast with its parts. Thus may be distinguished *tōtōs diēs* (e.g. Cic., *Dē fīn.*, 5, 74: *quīn etiam ipsī voluptāriī... virtūtēs habent in ōre tōtōs diēs*) = *all the days long* and *omnēs diēs* (e.g. Sen., *Dē brev. vītae*, 7.9: *ille... quī omnēs diēs tamquam vītam ōrdinat, nec optat crāstinum nec timet*) = *every single day*; Caes., *B.G.*, 6.5.1: *tōtus et mente et animō in bellum... īnsistit*; Cic., *Dē off.*, 1.18: *omnēs enim trahimur et dūcimur ad cognitiōnis et scientiae cupiditātem.* Cf. *mīlitēs tōtī in bellum irruērunt* = *the soldiers thew themselves completely (body and soul) into war* and *mīlitēs omnēs in bellum irruērunt* = *all the soldiers (leaving no one out) threw themselves into war.* Cic., *Or.*, 142: *ēloquentia... ōrnat... ūniversam rem pūblicam* = *eloquence adorns the whole state (as a complex, and not only in some of its parts).* *Cūnctus* will appear in chapter XXXII. In lines 82-85 of this chapter *tōtus mundus* indicates the world generically as an organic totality; *mundus ūniversus* contrasts with the divisions that the gods make in the world.

(53) *In hōc librō* has a different sense from *hōc librō*: the difference is like that, already described, between *in tōtā Italiā* and *tōtā Italiā*: the first is a true locative, the second is an ablative of means. The first can also refer only to a part of the book, while the second refers to the whole book.

Lēctiō secunda (56-108)

(57) The indirect reflexive *sibi* should be commented on: generally infinitival and subjunctive clauses will use *suus, suī, sibi* or *sē*, referring back to the main subject of the sentence (exceptions include result clauses and causal *cum* clauses).

(80) Here is an important meaning of *habēre* in the passive voice; *habērī* = *exīstimārī.*

(106) It should be noted that *dubitāstī* is the syncopated form of *dubitāvistī.* Other comparable forms may be generated as an in-class exercise: *amāstī, laudāstī, ōrāstī*, etc.

Lēctiō tertia (109-189)

(110) Students should commit to memory that *persuādēre* takes the dative: more examples at lines 115, 164, 173-174.

(143-144) The phrase *incidis in Scyllam, cupiēns vītāre Charybdim* goes back to the *Alexandreis* (5.301) of the fifteenth-century Latin poet Walter of Châtillon. It is commonly cited in the form *incidit in Scyllam quī vult vītāre Charybdim*" It corresponds to the Greek adage *tēn Chàrybdin ekphygōn tē Skýllē perièpesen*,

attested in Apostolius (16.49) and may be compared with our saying "from the frying pan into the fire." The *locus classicus* to which the teacher may refer is of course Book XII of Homer's *Odyssey*. Other Latin citations include Cic. *In Verrem āctiō secunda*, 5, 56, 146, Vergil's *Aeneid* 3.420-423, St. Jerome, *Ep.* 14, 6; 125, 2; 130, 7, Salvianus, *Dē gubernātiōne Deī*, 5, 11. In Christian authors Scylla and Charybdis represent the possibility of falling into two contrary sins, equally grave. The passage from Virgil cited above is noteworthy: *Aen.*, 3, 420 ss.: *Dextrum Scylla latus, laevum implācāta Charybdis / obsidet atque īmō barathrī ter gurgite vāstōs / sorbet in abruptum flūctūs rūrsusque sub aurās / ērigit alternōs et sīdera verberat undā./ At Scyllam caecīs cohibet spēlunca latebrīs / ōra exsertantem et nāvēs in saxa trahentem. / Prīma hominis faciēs et pulchrō pectore virgō / pūbe tenus, postrēma immānī corpore pistrīx / delphīnum caudās uterō commissa lupōrum.*

(1) Note the gerund of the verb *īre.*

(151-165) Students should take heed to memorize all the forms of *malle = magis velle* presented here.

(171) *Nēmō potest duōbus dominīs servīre* is drawn from Matth., 6, 24; *cf.*. Luc. 16, 13.

Capitulum XXIX: NAVIGARE NECESSE EST   cum + coniūnctīvus (76, 97), coniūnctīvus dubitātīvus 22, 23, 51 (first seen in 28. 184), interrogat/nescit num/quis 106, 117, 128, coniūnctīvus + ut/nē

Lēctiō prīma (1-59)

(9) Two negations in Latin amount to an affirmation: *nōnnūllī* thus means literally *not nobody*, which is to say, some people; similarly *nōnnumquam* in line 121 means *not never*, which is to say, once in a while. It may be added that, if the *nōn* precedes the negative form of the adjective, pronoun, or adverb, the affirmation is partial; if *nōn* follows, however, the affirmation is complete: *nōnnūllī = some*; *nūllī nōn* = 'there is no one who not' = 'everyone'; *nōnnumquam* = 'sometimes'; *numquam nōn* = 'it never happens that not' = 'always.'

(14) Note *eō cōnsiliō* proleptic to *ut* in the purpose clause. This is a fairly common usage in classical authors. E.g. Cic., *Dē fīn.*, 1, 21, 72: *Explicāvī sententiam meam, et eō quidem cōnsiliō, tuum iūdicium ut cognōscerem*; Caes., *B. G.*, 1, 48: *ultrā eum castra fēcit eō cōnsiliō, ut frūmentō commeātūque... Caesarem interclūderet*; Nep., *Milt.*, 5, 3: *proelium commīsērunt... hōc cōnsiliō, ut... montium altitūdine tegerentur*; Sall., *Cat.*, 57: *reliquōs Catilīna per montēs asperōs... in agrum Pistōriēnsem abdūcit eō cōnsiliō, ut per trāmitēs occultē perfugeret in Galliam Cisalpīnam.* Another example appears in lines 139-140.

(27) Students should recognize that *dīvitiae, -ārum* is a *plūrāle tantum*—a noun that appears only in the plural.

(38-43) The genitive plural of *noster* and *vester* is *nostrum, vestrum* when it has partitive force (= *ex nōbīs, ex vōbīs*) but *nostrī, vestrī* when it represents an objective genitive. Nevertheless with *omnis* the forms *omnium nostrum, omnium vestrum* are always used, regardless of the sense of the genitive, by a kind of attraction.

(45-51) The usage of *afficere* with the ablative of means in both the active and passive voices is worth emphasizing: *afficere aliquem laude, malō, beneficiō; afficī laude, morbō, dolōre.* There is another example at line 172 of this chapter.

(58-59) Here is introduced the indirect disjunctive in *utrum... an.*

Lēctiō secunda (60-126)

(62) Since animals are generally not conceived as agents but as means, in the phrase *delphīnō servātus est* the dolphin is in the ablative of means or instrument as in the phrase *Cornēlius equō vehitur.*

(71) It may be recalled here that the past participle of deponent verbs has an active force: *bēstiae ferae, nātūram suam oblītae...*

(72) Students should add *invidēre* to their inventory of special verbs that take the dative.

(75) Here is the adverb of motion from *inde.* It bears repeating that the *-n-* is characteristic of such adverbs: *inde, illinc, hinc, unde.*

(89) The chapter presents two idioms worthy of memorization: *dēspērāre vītam* and *dēspērāre dē salūte* (l. 120).

(99) *Hominem natantem subiit* as *rēgem Periandrum... adiit* in line 102 provide examples for discussing intransitive verbs that become transitive when compounded with prepositions and thus can also be used in the passive voice. Already in chapter XVI students encountered *adīre* with the accusative.

(116) Students should pay attention to the construction of *dubitāre* with an indirect interrogative introduced by *num. Verba dubitandī* can be construed with other interrogative particles or, more rarely, with an interrogative pronoun: Cic., *Dē rē p.*, 1, 38: *cūr igitur dubitās, quid dē rē pūblicā sentiās?*; Īd., *Dē off.*, 1, 3, 9: *honestumne factū sit an turpe, dubitant*; Nep., *Thrasybūl.*, 1: *sī per sē virtūs sine fortūnā ponderanda sit, dubitō, an hunc prīmum omnium pōnam*; Plin, *Ep.*, 6, 27, 1: *Dubitō, num idem tibi suādēre dēbeam*; Quint., 6, 1, 3: *licet et dubitāre num quid nōs fūgerit.* With *an* a positive response usually seems more plausible, with *num* the uncertainty is absolute.

(118) Note the use of the indicative with the disjunctive particles *sīve... sīve.*

(123-124) *Dum anima est, spēs est:* this phrase is drawn from a famous letter of Cicero *Att.*, IX, 10, 3: *Ut aegrōtō, dum anima est, spēs esse dīcitur, sīc ego, quoad Pompeius in Italiā fuit, spērāre nōn dēstitī:.* Cf. Ter., *Heaut.*, 98: *modo liceat vīvere est spēs;* the proverbial form is *Dum spīrō spērō.*

(123) Note the *ablātīvus quālitātis.*

Lēctiō tertia (127-202)

(153) Students should learn the idiomatic expressions *mīrum in modum* and *terribilem in modum* (177).

(161-162) Like *persuādēre* (encountered in chapter XXVIII) *suādēre* takes the dative. Where *tyrannō suāsit, ut iactūram faceret...* means, "he convinced the tyrant that he throw away...", *tyrannō suāsit iactūram esse faciendam...* would mean "he advised the tyrant that it was necessary to thow away..." Authors often observe this distinction between the construction of *suādēre* and *persuādēre* with accusative and infinitive = to persuade or convince that, and that with *ut* and the subjunctive = to advise to. E.g. Caes., *B. G.*, 1, 2: [*Orgetorīx*] *cīvitātī persuāsit, ut dē fīnibus suīs cum omnibus cōpiīs exīrent;* [*persuāsit item*] *perfacile esse, cum virtūte omnibus praestārent, tōtīus Galliae imperiō potīrī = Orgetorix advised all the inhabitants to leave their own territory en masse; he convinced them that it would be very easy to take possession of the rule of all Gaul, since they excelled everyone in martial valor.* In the marginal note *suādēre* is glossed as *= persuādēre cōnārī:* in fact the prefix *per-* gives the gives the compound verb a punctual aspect and a perfective sense. Cf. . Sen., *Ep.* 71, 30: *Suādeō mihi ista quae laudō, nōndum persuādeō = I try to convince myself of those things that I praise, but I have not yet convinced myself.*

(185) Students should understand *appropinquāre* takes the dative. Cf. *Cornēlius Iūliō appropinquat.* To move something towards something towards something else is usually expressed in Latin by *admovēre aliquid alicui.* A comprehensive review of verbs taking the dative is provided in *exercitium 7* of chapter XXXIV.

(187) As already noted in chapter XXVII on 108, *per* is here used in an exclamatory formula of adjuration: *per deōs immortālēs! Cf.* Cic., *Verr.*, 2, 3, 10, 25: *Per deōs immortālēs, quid est hoc?*; *ibīd.*, 35, 80: *Nam, per deōs immortālēs! quod dē capite iste dēmpsit, quō tandem modō vōbīs nōn modo ferendum, vērum etiam audiendum vidētur?* In this type of formula the interjection *prō* (sometimes spelled *prōh*, a different word from the preposition *prō*) commonly appears with the accusative of exclamation: *prō deum atque hominum fidem*, Ter., *And.*, 1, 5, 2, 11; Īd., *Heaut.*, 1, 1, 9; Cic., *Verr.*, 2, 3, 40, 137; Sall., *Cat.*, 20, 10. It may also be joined with a vocative as in Ter., *Ad.*, 2, 1, 42: *Prō suprēme Iuppiter!* Cic., *Phil.*, 2, 13, 32: *Prō sāncte Iuppiter!* In ROMA AETERNA students will encounter *Prō, Iuppiter!* at XL. 221. The accusative of exclamation often alternates with the vocative, as in line 198: *Ō dī bonī!*

(196) The idiom *magis magisque* means "more and more."

Capitulum XXX: CONVIVIUM futūrum perfectum (161-201); adverbium (-nter), coniūnctīvus hortātīvus 87, 120, numerī (singulī, bīnī...) 73-74

Lēctiō prīma (1-38)

(3) While students here read that Julius *vestem novam induit*, in line 15 they will read that he is *novā veste indūtus.* It may be pointed out that verbs like *induere, circumdare, dōnāre, aspergere* (109-111), *miscēre* (115 and 132) can take two constructions: *induō (mihi) vestem / induō mē veste; circumdō urbem mūrō / circumdō urbī mūrum; dōnō tibi librum / dōnō tē librō; aspergō cibum sale / aspergō cibō salem.* Compare also line 115 *Rōmānī vīnum cum aquā miscent* and line 132: *semper mel vīnō misceō. Circumdare* will be encountered in lines 19-21 of chapter XXXIII.

(16) Students should learn the common Latin salutation *salvēre tē iubeō.*

(17) After *ūtī* compare *fruī* with the ablative of means. There is another example in line 59.

(30) Point out that *docēre* with *dē* + abl. means "to inform about": *cf.* Cic., *Verr.*, 2, 4, 51: *dē eius iniūriīs iūdicēs docēre*; Īd., *Rōsc. Amer.*, 9, 26: *Ūsque adeō autem ille pertimuerat, ut morī māllet quam dē hīs rēbus Sullam docērī;* 44, 127: *Ego haec omnia Chrȳsogonum fēcisse dīcō,... ut hīs dē rēbus ā lēgātīs Amerīnōrum docērī L. Sullam passus nōn sit;* Sall., *Iug.*, 13, 3: *Adherbal... Rōmam lēgātōs mīserat, quī senātum docērent dē caede frātris et fortūnīs suīs.*

(33) Students should learn the construction of *praeesse* + dat. = 'to be in charge of', 'to supervise'. *Praeesse* can also be used in an absolute sense, with *in* + abl. *Cf.*, at line 81 of this chapter: *Uter nostrum in culīnā praeest?* Also, Cic., *Verr.*, 2, 3, 77, 180: *vidē, quaere, circumspice sī quis est forte ex eā prōvinciā, in quā tū triennium praefuistī.*

(35-36) Explain that *quod* in the phrase *prūdenter facis quod* is not strictly speaking causal, but substantive/declarative.

Lēctiō secunda (39-85)

(40-41) In the phrase *Sex hōrae sunt cum cibum nōn sūmpsī* the temporal *cum* has the sense of *ex quō* = there are six hours since = six hours have passed since.

(48) Note that *sitis, -is*, like a few other third declension nouns, has an accusative form in *-im* and the ablative in *-ī*.

(59) Here students may learn another Latin proverb: *Vīnum vīta est* and its variant *ex vīte vīta.*

(73) *Quot* is used here and not '*quotēnī convīvae in singulīs lectīs accubant?*', as one might expect from the distinction between *quot* e *quotēnī*: cf. H. Menge, *Repetitorium der lateinischen Syntax und Stilistik*, München, 1965, § 214, 14: *Quot discipulī in singulīs classibus (cf.* Quint., 1, 2, 23-24; 10, 5, 21) *scholae vestrae sunt?* '*Quotēnī*' is a very rare word which is not found in basic frequency lexica.

(78-79) Once again Latin uses the indicative where we might expect the conditional: '*Cēnam iam prīdem parātam esse oportuit!*'

Note the direct disjunctive in *-ne... an.*

Lēctiō tertia (86-158)

(129) Here *idem quod* is used in the same sense as *idem atque: Fabia... omnibus dē rēbus idem sentit quod marītus.*

(139) The tmesis of *ante... quam* is worth attention here: '*sententiam meam nōn ante dīcam quam utrumque gustāverō*' = '*sententiam meam nōn dīcam antequam utrumque gustāverō*'. Such usage is very common in classical authors: *cf.* e.g. Cic., *Phil.*, 11, 24: *ante prōvinciam sibi dēcrētam audiet quam potuerit tempus eī reī datum suspicārī;* Liv., 39, 10: *neque ante dīmīsit eum quam fidem dedit.*

(145) The phrase *cum prīmum meum vīnum pōtāveritis, Falernum pōtābitis* offers an opportunity to discuss the law of anteriority. Examples of this stylistic principle have appeared here from lines 83-84. More examples will appear in chapter XXXI.

(152) Reciprocity can be expressed by *inter sē* with no change in from active to passive voice. Cf. Ter., *Ad.*, 2, 4, 7: *quasi nunc nōn nōrimus inter nōs;* Cic., *Dīv.*, 1, 28, 58: *Saepe tibi meum nārrāvī... somnium: mē... vīdisse in quiēte... nōs inter nōs esse complexōs.*

Capitulum XXXI: INTER POCULA coniūnctīvus optātīvus (182, 183, 196 (next chapter 157, 183, 33.67, 71, 166 genitīvus quālitātis 101; gerundīvum (206-219)

Lēctiō prīma (1-58)

Aliquid can appear with a partitive genitive, as here *aliquid novī*, or with an adjective in agreement: *aliquid novum*. With third declension adjectives, however, agreement of adjectives is always observed: *aliquid turpe*. The same constructions apply to *nihil*.

(16) Here is introduced the construction of *quaerere* with *ā, ab* + abl. It is found again in line 36.

(29) Many examples of the law of anteriority appear in this chapter, as at lines 64, 65, 77-78, 102.

(38) Note the connecting relative construction *cui Orontēs*. Often at the beginning of a phrase *quī* is equivalent to *et is, et ille/ sed is, sed ille.*

A. The introduction of *simul atque* here, repeated at 44, provides an opportunity to review the different ways of saying *as soon as* that have been presented up to now: *cum prīmum, simul atque (simul ac)*. All of these constructions take the indicative. *Ubi prīmum* will be encountered at XXXII. 176.

(55-56) Students should learn that *fīdere* and *cōnfīdere* take the dative of the person but more often the ablative of the thing in which one trusts, although the dative also appears in this sense as at Verg., *Aen.*, 9, 378: *Celerāre fugam in silvās et fīdere noctī*; 11, 351: *Fugae fīdēns*; Ov., *Met.*, 15, 827: *Taedae nōn bene fīsa*; Tac., *Ann.*, 4, 59: *Praebuitque ipsī māteriem cūr amīcitiae cōnstantiaeque Seiānī magis fīderet. Cōnfīdere* is more commonly used in prose than *fīdere*, although the participle *fīdēns* does appear frequently.

Lēctiō secunda (59-131)

(69) Note the correlatives *tot... quot.*

(90) Students must remember that *ignōscere* takes the dative. Although contested by Ernout-Meillet, the explanation of the ancient grammarians is at least didactically useful: it was held that the prefix *in-* (*in-* + *gnōscere* □*ignōscere*) had a privative force (*cf.* the gloss *ignōscere: nōn nōscere*, Loewe, *Prodromus*, 409 e *Thēs. glōss. ēmend., s. v. ignōscō*), and thus that *ignōscere aliquid alicui* means "to not know (to pretend not to see) something for someone," with *alicui* as a *datīvus commodī* (dative of advantage).

Lēctiō tertia (132-204)

(140) The expressions *mittere/damnāre ad bēstiās* are worthy of attention.

(172) Regarding *fortissimus quisque*, it may be explained that the superlative followed by *quisque* means "all the most...", therefore *praestantissimus quisque* = 'all the most eminent'; *fortissimus quisque* 'all the bravest.' Cf. e.g. Cic., *Tūsc.*, 1, 31, 77: *Doctissimus quisque*; Caes., *B. G.*, 1, 45: *Antīquissimum quodque tempus*; and also in the plural: Plaut., *Mōst.*, 1, 76: *Optimī quīque expetēbant ā mē doctrīnam sibi.*

(176) Like all reduplicated forms and composite forms in *cumque*, *quisquis* generally takes the indicative, though we might expect a subjunctive in English.

(179) In reading aloud one should pause between *ūnum* and *tantum* to show that *tantum* is correlated with *quantum* and not taken together with *tē ūnum*. The expression *alterum tantum* means "two times as much," like the Greek *héteron tosoúton*: cf. Plaut., *Epid.*, 3, 81: *Etiamsī alterum tantum perdendum est, perdam potius quam sinam*; Cic., *Ōr.*, 56, 188: *Alterō tantō longior.*

(185-186) The proverbial expression *ab ōvō ūsque ad māla* comes from Horace (*Sat.*, 1, 3, 6 e s.) and refers to the Roman custom of beginning with an hors d'oeuvre where often an egg was served, and ending with fruit. The expression thus means generally "from beginning to end."

38

Capitulum XXXII: CLASSIS ROMANA coniūnctīvus perf. 226-273, cum + coniūnctīvus 176, next chapter **109; genetīvus + oblivīscī/meminisse 126, 156, nē –eris! 162, 183, 199, 211, 215, 243, 254, perfectum coni. 226-273**

Lēctiō prīma (1-59)

Cūnctus is explained in the note as equivalent to *omnis* or *tōtus* in the singular, but to *omnēs* in the plural, where *cūnctus* emphasizes the union of the parts; *cf.* Paul. Fest., 44 Linds.: '*Cūnctī*' *sīgnificat quidem omnēs, sed coniūnctī et congregātī.* Other examples of *cūnctus / cūnctī* appear in lines 40, 43, 53.

(41) Another example of *afficere* accompanied by an ablative which conveys its meaning to the verb: *summīs laudibus affēcit* = 'he praised him in an extraordinary manner,' he conferred the greatest praises on him.'

(49) Note the *ablātīvus quālitātis* first seen at XXIX.123.

Lēctiō secunda (60-129)

(60) This passage reinforces the practical rule of the indirect reflexive, according to which *suus* and *sē* are used in phrases with the infinitive and the subjunctive. More examples at lines 142-143 and 147.

(66-69) Here is an opportunity to learn two more Latin proverbs: *fortēs Fortūna (ad)iuvat*, found in Terence (*Phorm.*, 203), Cicero (*Dē fīn.*, 3, 4, 16; *cf. Tūsc.*, 2, 4, 11), Livy (8, 29, 5; 34, 37, 4) and the younger Pliny (*Ep.* 6, 16, 11). Virgil (*Aen.*, 10, 284) uses *audentēs Fortūna iuvat*, as do Ovid (*Met.*, 10, 586; *Ars am.*, 1, 606; *Fāstī*, 2, 782), Seneca (*Ep.* 94, 28), Claudianus (*Carm. Minōra*, 41, 9) and Corippus (*Iōhann.*, 6, 711). The other is taken from the Gospel *Converte gladium tuum in locum suum* (Matth., 26, 52), better known in the formulation of John (18, 11): *Mitte gladium tuum in vāgīnam.* Better known is the rest of the phrase as related by Matthew: *Omnēs... quī accēperint gladium gladiō perībunt*, simplified as *Quī gladiō ferit gladiō perit.*

(72) *Dōnec*, which is fairly rare in Cicero (only four usages, and always with the sense 'up until the moment at which') and completely absent from Caesar, nevertheless appears with some frequency in Augustan poetry and in Livy. With the meaning 'for all the time that' it, like *dum* with the same meaning, generally takes the indicative for all tenses. Thus *vīvam* here is, naturally, future. Another example, drawn from Ovid (*Trīst.*, 1, 9, 5) is at line 104.

(74) Here is the construction *petere* with *ā, ab* + abl. It is worth reviewing all the sense of *petere* and the constructions with words of asking generally—*repetītiō est māter studiōrum* and *repetīta iuvant.* Other examples of *petere* appear in lines 88 and 120. In line 169 appears the construction *postulāre ab aliquō aliquid.*

Observe that *dissuādēre* governs the dative like *suādēre* e *persuādēre*; it can appear with *nē* + subj. and, more often, with the infinitive (with or without the accusative.) *cf.* Gell., 7, 2: *Is mē dēhortātur dissuādetque nē bellum faciam*; anche C. Gracch. *apud* Gell., 11, 10: *Quī prōdeunt dissuāsūrī nē hanc lēgem accipiātis*; Cic., *Dē off.*, 3, 27, 101: *Quī nōn modo nōn cēnsuerit captīvōs remittendōs, vērum etiam dissuāserit*; Sen., *Herc. Oet.*, 929: *Quīcumque miserae dissuādet morī crūdēlis est*; Quint., 4, 2, 121: *Nē sententiā quidem stomachum iūdicis reficere dissuāserim*; Īd., 2, 8, 7: *Certum studiōrum facere dēlēctum nēmō dissuāserit*; Suet.,

Tīb., 2: *Appius Caecus societātem cum rēge Pyrrhō, ut parum salūbrem, inīrī dissuāsit.*

(78) *Opus est* is here introduced in its construction with the ablative of means (up to now it has been used only with the infinitive.) It is worth pointing out that *opus est* can also have a personal construction: one can say '*Quid opus est armīs?*' or '*Quid opus sunt arma?*': *cf.*, e.g., Plaut., *Capt.*, 1, 61: *Maritimī mīlitēs opus sunt tibi*; Cic., *Fam.*, 2, 6, 1: *Huius nōbīs exempla permulta opus sunt*; Liv., 1, 41, 1: *Quae cūrandō vulnerī opus sunt.* The person who has need is put in the dative case: *mihi opus est aliquā rē / mihi opus est aliqua rēs. Opus est* indicates a subjective need, linked to individual will or to utility, and thus contrasts to objective absolute necessity, and also contrasts with indigence of something, which is expressed by *necesse est* or by *egēre* and *indigēre*: *cf.* e.g. Cato *apud* Sen., *Ep.* 94, 28: *Emās nōn quod opus est, sed quod necesse est*; Sen., *Ep.* 9, 12: *Ait [Chrᵢsippus] sapientem nūllā rē indigēre, tamen multīs illī rēbus opus esse, contrā stultō nūllā rē opus est, nūllā rē enim ūtī scit, sed omnibus eget.* As the last example shows, *opus est* is strictly related to the capacity of *ūtī.* In fact, not only do both *ūtī* and *opus est* take the ablative of means, but *opus est* alternates with *ūsus est* already in authors of the classical period: *cf.* Ter., *Heaut.*, 1, 28-29: *M.: Mihi sīc est ūsus; tibi ut opus factō est, face. Ch.: An cuiquam est ūsus hominī, sē ut cruciet? M.: Mihi.* The construction of *opus est* with the ablative of the perfect participle will be presented in *ROMA AETERNA.* There are further examples of *opus est* with the ablative in lines 118 and 195. In line 124 it is used absolutely: *sī opus fuerit.*

(84) Following on *dubitāre num* here we find *haud sciō an.*

(86-90) The so-called "law of anteriority" is not a fixed rule that must be applied every time that one action is logically and abstractly prior to another, but only when the writer or speaker wants to express this circumstance. Furthermore, it is not enough that an action be begun, but it must also be completed before the next one. For example, in the phrase *Fēlīx eris, sī pecūniae grātiā vītae tuae parcent*, the two verbal processes are seen as contemporaneous. The famous Ovidian distich at lines 104-105 may be helpful in this regard. The first verse represents two durative verbal processes seen as parallel: many friends are numbered over the whole time when one is fortunate; in the second verse, however, the change of circumstance is presented as a prior and completed fact, after which one is left alone.

Lēctiō tertia (130-224)

(146) Like *eō cōnsiliō* as already seen, here *hāc condiciōne* is proleptic in relation to *ut.*

B. Students should remember that *minārī* takes the dative.

(175) The introduction of *cum* in the concessive sense = although presents an opportunity to review the concessive constructions encountered up to now: *etsī*, and *quamquam* with the indicative; *cum* with the subjunctive.

(175-176) Another locution for "as soon as": *ubi prīmum.*

(176-177) Students should notice how Latin often renders in a single phrase including a participle that which we might more naturally express with two coordinated constructions: *Captōs praedōnēs in crucem tollī iussit* = "he captured the pirates and ordered that they be crucified." Likewise lines 212-213 *Timeō nē mē captum Rōmam abdūcant* would naturally be rendered into English as "I fear lest they capture me and take me to Rome." Otherwise *Lȳdia ānulum oblātum accipit* can only be rendered, "Lydia took the ring that was offered to her."

(189) The *quod* that follows *ignōsce mihi* is not actually causal but substantive: originally it was a neuter accusative of the relative pronoun understood as an accusative of relation— "as for the fact that I accused you, pardon me!"

Capitulum XXXIII: EXERCITUS ROMANUS *sī/nisi + coni. 73-76, 82-85, 208-214, 220-225, coniūnctīvus irreālis (73-76, 82, 85, 181-182, 208-214) coniūnctīvus plūsquamperf. 194-236; gerundīvum/gerundium (80, 94-98, 116), imperātīvus futūrī 237-248; numerī (singulī, bīnī…) 2-3; plūsquamperfectum coni. 194-236*

Lēctiō prīma (1-47)

Accurate study of this chapter will enable students to read without great difficulty much of the works of Caesar and other authors who treat martial subjects without great difficulty. Accordingly it is advisable to spend all the time necessary for a full assimilation of the vocabulary and phraseology in this unit.

(18-19) Note the double nominative in the phrase *Dux ā mīlitibus 'imperātor' salūtātur.*

Here *locō... idōneō* is equivalent to *in locō idōneō*: the preposition is dispensable because the local sense is clear from the noun

(20) Here students meet the verb *circúmdare*: it should be noted that this verb governs the same double constructions as *induere, dōnāre* and other verbs analyzed in chapter XXX. Thus one can say both *castra vāllō et fossā circumdantur* and *castrīs vāllum et fossa circumdantur*. Students should pay attention to pronounce this verb *circúmdare* and not *circumdáre*.

Another verb that takes the dative: *studēre.*

Students should memorize the useful idiom *stipendia merēre.*

Lēctiō secunda (48-104)

(65) The primary meaning of *dēsīderāre* is 'to feel the absence of,' with the basic idea of having lost something that one would like to get back. In the technical language of philology *quaedam verba dēsīderantur* means 'some words have been lost' = are missing. Cf. 137: *haud multī dēsīderantur.*

(77-79) Note the impersonal construction of *decet.*

(91) In the plural *litterae, -ārum* indicates either a single letter or missive (*ūnae litterae = ūna epistula*) or several such letters (*bīnae, trīnae, quaternae litterae = duae, trēs, quattuor epistulae*): cf. Cic., *Fam.*, 3, 7: *Ūnīs litterīs tōtīus aetātis rēs gestās ad senātum perscrībere; ibīd.*, 10, 18: *Bīnīs continuīs litterīs ut ventrem rogāvit. Epistula* is the letter in the material sense, while *litterae* refers rather to its content; cf. Cic., *ad Q. fr.*, 3, 1, 3: *Veniō ad tuās litterās, quās plūribus epistulīs accēpī*, 'I come to your writings, which I received in several letters/installments' (*epistula* is from the Greek *epistéllō* = I send to). It is important to recall that with *plūrālia tantum* and with nouns like *litterae* that have a different sense in the plural from the singular one uses distributive instead of cardinal numbers, and in particular *ūnī* and *trīnī* instead

of *singulī* and *ternī.*

(101) Students should take care to distinguish the perfect form *cecīdī* from *cecidī < cadere*, and also in its composite forms: *occīdō < caedere*, but *occido < cadere; incīdō/incido*, etc.

Lēctiō tertia (105-192)

(116) Here one may review the different ways of expressing purpose encountered up to now: *ut* + subj.; *ad* + gerund/gerundive; *causā* and *grātiā* + gen. of the gerund/gerundive; the supine (with verbs of motion; there is a new example in this chapter at line 150).

(143-144) The subjunctive is used here instead of the indicative because the thought and speech of the *dux* is being reported, as indicated by the quotation marks: "He praised our valor, because he thought that we had fought with great courage." It is not said or implied that Aemilius does not share this opinion, but the statement is simply attributed to him. In other contexts a certain detachment from the reported thought is clear from the context: *Athēniēnsēs Sōcratem damnāvērunt, quod iuvenēs corrūpisset*, "The Athenians condemned Socrates, on the pretext that he had corrupted the young."

C. Note the construction *gaudēre aliquā rē.*

(173) Compare *etiam atque etiam* with the already encountered idiom *magis magisque.*

Capitulum XXXIV: DE ARTE POETICA

This chapter presents an opportunity to speak of lyric poetry and Latin epigram. Our own practice is to ask students to commit verses to memory, which they may then assimilate and recite in class.

Lēctiō prīma (1-58)

(17-18) The construction *dummodo* + subjunctive (volitive: in fact the negative form takes *nē*) = 'provided that.'

(25) *Plūs* often appears without *quam*: cf. Ter., *Ad.*, 2, 46: *Plūs quīngentōs colaphōs īnfrēgit mihi*; Cic., *Dē rē p.*, 2, 22, 40: *Nōn plūs mīlle quīngentōs*; Liv., 31, 34: *Paulō plūs ducentōs passūs ā castrīs.*

(37) Note the construction with *iuvāre: Lūdī circēnsēs mē nōn minus iuvant quam gladiātōriī*. Take the opportunity to review all the impersonal verbs encountered up to now: *decet, fallit, iuvat.* More will be encountered in *ROMA AETERNA.*

(40) Another verb that takes the dative, *favēre* + dat.— here it has the sense, "to be a fan of." *Exercitium 7* in *EXERCITIA LATINA*(pag. 273) provides a useful review of these special verbs.

(47) Here for the first time students encounter the atemporal use of *dum* with the present. The instructor may explain that when *dum* means "while, at the same time as" it always takes the present indicative, without regard for the tense of the main verb. It may be helpful for students to memorize the famous phrase of Livy 21, 7, 1: *Dum ea Rōmānī parant, iam Saguntum summā vī oppugnābātur* (this locus is best known in its proverbial form: *Dum Rōmae cōnsulitur, Saguntum expugnātur*) Many other examples will be found in *ROMA AETERNA.*

(57) This guide will not address the metrical reading of verses; most grammars provide discussion of scansion, and practical

guidebooks are available (e.g. J.W. Halporn, M. Ostwald, T.G. Rosenmeyer, *The Meters of Greek and Latin Poetry*, University of Oklahoma Press, Norman, 1980). Nonetheless the comments of G.B. Pighi on this subject may be of interest (G. B. Pighi, *Quōmodo versūs legendī sint*, in: *Dē librō Aenēidos VI, quae est catabasis Aenēae*, Pontificium Athēnaeum Salesiānum, Rōmae, 1967, pagg. 139-144): "'*Scandere*' *nihil aliud esse quam versūs recitāre quī crēdunt, iī quidem tōtō caelō, ut aiunt, errant. Nempe in scholīs Rōmānīs, postquam longitūdinēs et brevitātēs distinguī dēsitae sunt et intentiōrēs syllabae fierī coepērunt, quae ōlim ēlātiōrēs fuerant, discipulī, ut pedēs discerent, versum dīvidere iussī sunt. Ita Prīsciānus in* Partītiōne XII *versuum Aenēidos*, gramm. *III pp. 461 ss.*: scande versum: armavi rumqueca nōtro iaequī [cioè *nōtroj iaequī*, due spondei: v. *Phōnētica Latīna*, pag. 282, in principio] prīmusab ōrīs... scande versum: conticu ēreom nēsin tentī quōrate nēbant; atque aliī ármavi, aliī armaví ēnūntiābant. Quae legendī ratiō fuit nūlla, sed omnīnō versum dīvidendī. Sed cum renāscentium litterārum temporibus Graecōs Latīnōsque versūs novellīs linguīs imitārī doctī virī vellent, fuērunt, in Germāniā praesertim, quī scansiōnem continuam, ut est* ármavirúmquecanó, *sibi ad imitandum prōpōnerent: ita factum est illud versuum 'barbarōrum' genus, quod Theodiscīs māximē placuit atque, ut nostrātem nōminem, Iōannī Pascoli. Neque tamen ea fuit 'metrica' versificātiō, ut quīdam falsō opīnantur, sed 'syllabica' et 'accentiōnum' (vocābulō ūtitur Favōnius Eulogius* somn. Scīp. *p. 15, 15 Holder) ōrdine quōdam cōnsistēns, ut sunt plērumque recentiōrum linguārum versificātiōnēs... Sequitur ut Latīnī versūs ita legendī sint ut nostrōs legimus, dummodo syllabās longās nē corripiāmus, brevēs nē prōdūcāmus, nēve intentiōrem faciāmus quae ēlātior fuerit. Hic est, quod ad nōs attinet, nōdus, quī nostrīs quidem linguīs et ōribus vix et aegrē expedīrī potest. Nam facile adsuēscimus longās brevēsque rēctē ēnūntiāre ac distinguere, sed Rōmāna cantilēna abhinc mīlle quīngentōs annōs obmūtuit: quamquam exaudīre possumus in Ambrosiānīs et Grēgoriānīs antīquissimīs cantibus. Necesse est igitur ut accentūs nostrōs quam māximē extenuēmus, ex quibus abnōrmis et prōrsus aliēnus rhythmus nāscātur, atque ut dīligentissimē mēnsūram syllabārum servēmus: hoc sī fēcerimus, ipsōs Vergiliī versūs suō rhythmō, suō quasi sonō praeditōs licēbit audīre: quōs nōn est dubium quīn haec nostra loquendī cōnsuētūdō aliquantulum vexet et vitiet, sed ipsam versūs animam, rhythmum dīcō, sōspitātam laetābimur*" (pagg. 140 e s.). It may be argued that, if we cannot reproduce the vowel quantity and musical accent of ancient poetry, it is better to read verses as though they were prose, rather than distributing word accents in an arbitrary manner. The problem of ancient prosody is complex and cannot be addressed in this manual.

Lēctiō secunda (59-154)

(114) For metrical reasons one should read here *ūnius* as a proparoxytone (accent on the antepenult *únius*) and not the paroxytone *ūnīus* (penult accent *uníus*). Line 121 presents a contrasting example, where one should read *fēcerīmus* (*fecerímus*) and not *fēcerimus* (*fecérimus*).

(125-126) Students should understand the difference between *uxōrem dūcere* and *nūbere*. The former is said of the man, the latter (which strictly means "to take the veil for..."— *nūbere* has the same root as *nūbēs*) is said of the woman, and takes the dative. Lines 191-193 present another example of the two verbs.

Lēctiō tertia (155-217)

Capitulum XXXV: ARS GRAMMATICA *nōmen 7-37, genus nōminis (13-18); numerus singulāris/plūrālis (19-22), cāsus 19-28, positīvus (gradus) 33, prōnōmen 38-56, persōnae 50-53, 97-100, genus verbī (65-81); passīvum 72-74, numerus singulāris/plūrālis verbī 82-85, participium 127-154, coniūnctio 155-175; praepositiō (176-213), praepositiōnēs + acc. 181-193, praepositiōnēs + abl. 194-199, praepositiōnēs + acc. 181-193, praepositiōnēs + abl./acc. 200-313, interiectiō (214-221), dēclīnātiōnēs I-V 224-231; coniugātiōnēs I-IV 232-237,*

Lēctiō prīma (1-56)
Lēctiō secunda (57-221)

The first volume of the course concludes with this chapter, which consists in a long *excerptum* from the *Ars minor* of Aelius Donatus, the Roman grammarian of the fourth century who was the teacher of St. Jerome. This books had great success throughout the middle ages and was memorized in schools (see L. Holtz, *Donat et la tradition de l'enseignement grammatical*, Paris, 1981). For us it serves as a rapid but effective review of the fundamental rules of morphology. Students who have read with diligence all the volume *FAMILIA ROMANA* from the first to the last chapter have all the means at their disposal to rapidly reach the goal of fluent and appreciative reading of the Latin classics. By now students have learned virtually all the principal forms and structures of the language of Rome and have assimilated more than 1,500 of the most basic words in Latin vocabulary. On this basis they can already read texts of moderate difficulty, such as those presented in the last chapters of *FAMILIA ROMANA* and in the first chapters of *ROMA AETERNA*. They are prepared to read, with the help of an instructor, Ørberg's edition of Plautus's *Amphitryō*, of *Caesaris Bellum Gallicum* and of a large anthology of ancient authors (*Sermones Romani*), illustrated with marginal notes and glosses in the same manner as *FAMILIA ROMANA*, . Presentation of this work in dramatic form can be an excellent exercise. Students should also now have the ability to speak and write in Latin, to the extent this is useful for reading the ancient authors. They must persevere to the authors themselves. This will be achieved, with the gradualism characteristic of this course, in the volume *ROMA AETERNA. Pergānt fortiter!*

APPENDIX I: ADVICE TO THE TEACHER

Before starting to read a new chapter the students should study the picture heading the chapter or the map facing the first page. Through a brief English discussion the teacher may help them to observe important details and to familiarize themselves with the theme or the setting, without entering upon the actual content of the text. In any case the preliminary discussion in English, if practiced, should not take more than a few minutes.

In the presentation of the text itself only Latin should be used. The object is to accustom the students, from the start, to read and understand the Latin text as Latin without the interference of English, or with a minimum interference of English. Begin by reading the text aloud, making the whole class or (later) individual students echo each sentence. If the reading is done carefully, with correct pronunciation and appropriate accentuation and grouping of words, the students will find to their satisfaction that they can understand the text immediately and will feel no need to translate.

Pronunciation will be taught by encouraging the students to imitate their teacher, who must therefore take great pains to pronounce as correctly and distinctly as possible.

When listening to and repeating the sentences, the students should normally have their books open before them, or have the pages shown on transparencies, so that they can see the written word at the same time.

It is important for the teacher, when first presenting the text, to know exactly what words and what grammatical forms and structures are new to the students. The *self-explanatory* text assures that the meaning of every new word and the function of every new grammatical form can be understood from the context, but a lively presentation, with suggestive intonation and gesturing and with frequent reference to visual aids, will always be a great help to the students. Their spontaneous response will generally be sufficient to show that they have grasped everything, while on the other hand an occasional puzzled look or failure to respond will reveal difficulties. In such cases, and whenever you want to be on the safe side, you can make the meaning clear by repeating one or two sentences with special stress on the word or form in question, or by illustrating the point with further examples or drawings. The same procedure can be used to call students' attention to new grammatical features.

After a passage has been presented in this way, individual students may be asked to take turns to read parts of the passage aloud in a manner that shows understanding through correct phrasing and accentuation. If the passage contains dialogue, parts can be assigned to different students (the teacher or a student can act as narrator). This is one way of checking the students' comprehension of the text. But to make quite sure that the passage

has been precisely understood and assimilated, various other procedures must be used.

First of all you can ask simple questions in Latin concerning the content of the passage just studied (detailed questions on each lesson can be found in the volume *EXERCITIA LATINA*). Some of the questions may be accompanied by the showing of pictures. When answering the questions the students should normally be allowed to keep their books open, so that if necessary they can find the answer in the book (the very fact that they can spot the right answer shows that they understand the meaning of both question and answer).

In the last resort, if you are still in doubt whether a new word or a new grammatical form has been correctly understood by everybody, you may ask one of the students to give an English equivalent. However, if the text is carefully presented with proper emphasis on new features, translation, whether of single words or whole sentences, will generally be felt to be superfluous. Of course the English translations of Latin words and phrases will often be present in the students' minds, but when reading the text they should be encouraged to concentrate on understanding the Latin directly as it stands instead of searching for English equivalents. The very fact that they are not asked to translate will help them to such direct understanding, which is prerequisite for obtaining proficiency in reading and insight into the mechanism of the language and its means of expression (The general comprehension of the text may be checked by asking a student to give an English paraphrase.)

Most teachers will find it necessary to explain and discuss points of grammar in English on the lines of the *instructions* given in the Students' Manual *LATINE DISCO*. When this is practiced, the formulation of rules should preferably be left to the students themselves after they have seen several examples of the grammatical forms functioning in context.

As a further help to observe and learn the grammatical system, each chapter is followed by a grammar section, *GRAMMATICA LATINA*, which contains systematically arranged examples of the new points of grammar with the relevant Latin grammatical terms. Since the teacher will probably already have called attention to most of these points, the study of this section need not take up much time.

The chapters of *LINGVA LATINA* are so long that they will have to be divided into several lessons. The division into lessons *(lectiones)* shown in the margin by roman numerals *(I, II, III),* and followed in *EXERCITIA LATINA*, is intended as a guide for the teacher, but more than one period will be needed for some of the lessons. However, in the interest of promoting the reading skill the teacher should not make the readings too short.

The three PENSA at the end of each chapter constitute the

---

20   Reprinted by the kind permission of the author.

final test of the students' comprehension of the material taught in the chapter. After studying both the main text and the *GRAMMATICA LATINA* section, the students are required to copy the PENSA (as homework or in class), filling in grammatical endings in PENSVM A, and new words in PENSVM B (special PENSA forms with blanks to be filled in are provided in the Teacher's Materials). The questions in PENSVM C should be answered with complete sentences, but if this has already been done orally in class, written answers need not be given. If these exercises are done satisfactorily (with at least some 80 per cent of the answers correct), this is the best guarantee that the whole chapter, with its new grammar and vocabulary, has been understood and assimilated by the students. Whenever reinforcement of certain points is needed, the more detailed exercises in *EXERCITIA LATINA* can be used. (Keys to the PENSA and *EXERCITIA* are available for teachers who want them.)

In spite of careful reviewing students will, as they progress in their reading, come across some words whose meaning they have forgotten. In most cases the teacher can help a student out by giving an example of the word used in an easy context which clarifies the meaning; but the students can also find out the meaning for themselves by consulting the INDEX VOCABVLORVM at the end of the volume. The teacher should show the students, when they have read one or two chapters, how they can use the reference to chapter and line to find the passage where the word occurs for the first time in a context which will generally be sufficient to make the meaning clear. (This effort is more rewarding than looking up the word in the *Latin-English Vocabulary*). In a similar way the treatment of grammatical points can be retraced by means of the INDEX GRAMMATICVS (pp. 326-327).

HANS H. ØRBERG

APPENDIX II: SAMPLE LESSON PLANS FROM IAN THOMSON,

TEACHER'S MANUAL (1975)[20]

SAMPLE LESSON PLANS
CAPITVLVM PRIMVM

Lesson analysis

1. lines 1-15: Introduction of *est* and *sunt; in* + abl. *-ā* of lst decl. sing.; *et, quoque, nōn, sed; -ne* and *ubi* introducing questions; proper names: *Rōma, Italia, Eurōpa, Graecia, Hispānia, Aegyptus, Āfrica, Gallia, Syria, Asia, Arabia, Germānia, Britannia.*

2. lines 16-37: Introduction of nominatives *fluvius* and *fluviī, īnsula* and *īnsulae, oppidum* and *oppida;* principle of adjectival agreement via *magnus* and *parvus;* proper names: *Nīlus, Rhēnus, Dānuvius, Tiberis, Corsica, Sardinia, Sicilia, Melita, Brundisium, Tūsculum, Sparta, Delphī.*

3. lines 38-61: Introduction of *num* (inviting negative response) and *quid;* reinforcement of grammar and vocabulary; *in* + abl. *-ō* of 2nd decl. sing. n.; new vocabulary: *Graecus, Rōmānus, multī, paucī, imperium, prōvincia;* proper names: *Crēta, Rhodus, Naxus, Samos, Chios, Lesbos, Lēmnos, Euboea, ōceanus Atlanticus.*

4. lines 62—83: New examples of lst and 2nd decl. nouns and adjectives in the nom.: *littera -ae, numerus -ī, vocābulum -a, syllaba -ae; prīmus, secundus, tertius, Latīnus, capitulum, mīlle, sex, ūnus;* other vocabulary items: *ɪ, ɪɪ, ɪɪɪ, A, B, C, D, E, F.*

5. lines 84-106 (GRAMMATICA LATINA): Formal exposition of grammar: nom. sing. and plur. of lst and 2nd decl. nouns and adjectives; vocabulary: *grammatica, singulāris, plūrālis, exemplum.*

Materials required for Cap. I: Wall map (or transparency) of Roman Empire with Latin names; transparencies of pp. 7 and 8.

Lesson 1

(1) Organizational procedures:

introduce self, identify textbook, etc. *Note:* Direct method purists sometimes begin the exclusive use of Latin immediately (*"ego magister/magistra sum, vōs discipulī estis,* etc.), but this is not recommended. Students should gradually over the first few lessons be keyed into the method. Too much material thrown out with inadequate explanation of what is happening will tend to confuse and alienate students.

(2) Brief introduction to the Method.

The teacher explains that in this class the rules that govern the Latin language will not be formally stated beforehand or consciously memorized, but learned naturally by reading passages of connected Latin. The aim of the course is to get students to the point where they can read and immediately understand Latin passages of ordinary difficulty without English words coming into their heads. For this purpose translation into idiomatic English will not be called for, and only rarely will English equivalents for Latin words be mentioned. The use of English for giving instructions and explicating difficulties is not forbidden, but it will steadily be replaced by Latin, until Latin is almost exclusively used in class.

In this course students learn by doing. For example, correct pronunciation is learned by imitating the teacher. Students will also have the chance to deduce the meanings of all new words for themselves, because the text is devised to be *self-explanatory.* A great many exercises, both oral and written, will give students practice in applying what they have learned and a constant check on their progress. Exercises will be done in class and at home. If these are done carefully, total mastery of all material in the textbook can be achieved. (Further discussion of the Method is probably undesirable at this stage.)

(3) Introduce map of IMPERIVM ROMANVM. Teacher points to each name on map, *Rōma, Italia, Graecia, Hispānia, Eurōpa,* modeling the pronunciation of each for imitation by students. Insist on a strong, confident-sounding response in full chorus, but ignore all but the most serious errors in pronunciation: it is more important at this stage that students lose their fears and inhibitions. Still without showing the text, teacher instructs students to listen (in Latin and English: *"Audīte, listen!"*) and reads the first paragraph through aloud, pointing to locations on the map as they are mentioned. The pace should not be too slow. Teacher models each sentence three or four times for full choral repetition, using instructions to repeat in both Latin and English (*"Reddite!* repeat!" and *"Iterum!* again!"*: see Appendix A). Teacher then shows lst paragraph (lines 1-4) on overhead projector and instructs students, in both Latin and English, to repeat each sentence after the teacher.

Model each sentence as many times as it takes to elicit a confident response.

The above process should take about 5 minutes.

(4) Teacher reads the second paragraph (lines 5-10) aloud following the same procedure as above without showing the text. Teacher then unmasks the paragraph and models for student repetition, still giving commands in both Latin and English. When full choral repetition is finished, teacher divides class into choral groups, (e.g. boys, girls, halves of the room) to read the paragraph through without the teacher's model. If the reading is thin and straggling, model several times for repetition in full chorus.

Follow same procedure for paragraph 3 (lines 11-15). Finally, using both paragraphs, teacher conducts rapid chain drill, each student in turn reading a sentence aloud. If a student has difficulty, teacher models the sentence for full choral repetition several times. If available, a tape-recording should sometimes be substituted for the teacher's model. About 10 minutes.

Notes: (a) For the first week or so corrections should be made with the entire class repeating the correct form; even when only one student reveals a difficulty, there are likely to be others with the same problem who have not revealed it or who may even be unaware that they have a difficulty. (b) The progression has been from choral repetition without the printed word to choral repetition with the printed word to partial choral repetition to individual reading.

(5) Students now read from their books the material (lines 1-15) which was shown on transparencies. For instructions — in both Latin and English — to open books and read aloud in full chorus.

(6) The remaining 15 or 20 minutes should be devoted to Exercitia 1-3, which cover all the material contained in lines 1-15. The easiest way for the teacher is to read Exercitia 1 aloud letting students finish each sentence chorally, and to prepare a transparency of Exercitiium 2 and use the overhead projector, unmasking each sentence as it is required. There is, however, some danger of boring students by using the same device too frequently. Variety of presentation can be achieved by using flash cards with one sentence on each, or by distributing individual copies of the EXERCITIA LATINA, or by displaying them written on the blackboard. In the last case the teacher should have prepared the blackboard before class and kept the Exercitia concealed until needed. Teacher calls for volunteers to do each sentence. If a correction is necessary, teacher will shake head (possibly adding *perperam* 'wrong') and model correct response for full choral repetition twice. The number of repetitions required can be indicated by the language cue *bis,* with teacher holding up two fingers and translating the cue. Here, as always, every possible reinforcement of the meaning of the Latin should be used.

If time permits, finish by asking questions on lines 1-15 like those suggested in Exercitium 3.

Assignments: (a) Read lines 1-15 aloud at least three times. (b) Draw a map, writing in all names contained in lines 1-15.

Lesson 2

(1) Collect homework, which should be returned no later than next lesson period. (On grading policies, see Part I, § 13.)

(2) Introduce lines 16-26. Follow procedures described in Lesson 1. About 10 minutes.

(3) Students read lines 18-26 from books. teacher selects individuals to read (for command involved, see Appendix A). Corrections repeated twice in full chorus. This should take only 3-5 minutes.

(4) Explanations are most effective when their content is needed and usable. This is therefore a good moment to discuss, in English, the value and use of the illustrations and marginalia. Teacher explains that new words and forms (it may be necessary to define this term) are introduced in such a way that their meanings and functions appear clearly from the context or from illustrations or explanations in the margin. This will help students associate Latin words directly with the object or notion they describe. It should be emphsized that illustrations and marginal information are there for the convenience of the student, not the teacher. As examples of this, discuss the illustration on page 1 and the symbol of opposition (↔) in the margin opposite line 23. Teacher now invites questions about the Method. Keep replies as clear and uncomplicated as possible. Students appreciate some explanation of what the teacher is doing and why, and tend to work more happily as a result. This discussion should take about 10 minutes, but can be prolonged if students display serious misunderstandings or raise really useful questions. An experienced teacher will know when students begin to side-track.

(5) Introduce lines 27-37 from book, using map in book or wall map to illustrate. If map in book is used, teacher reads each sentence, class repeats in chorus and finds locations on map, teacher reads sentence again, class repeats twice. If wall map is used, teacher points to locations. 5-7 minutes.

If any time remains, have students point on wall map to various locations in response to questions such as *Ubi est Arabia? Estne Aegyptus in Asiā?* etc. (see Exercitium 3).

Assignment: Review all material so far covered. Practice aloud, reading each paragraph at least three times.

Lesson 3

(1) Return and comment on work previously handed in. Hereafter this procedure will not be mentioned in the lesson plans, but teachers should allow for it. Normally no more than 5 minutes will be required.

(2) Class does Exercitium 4 orally. The singular and plural endings should be pronounced very distinctly and the agreement between the endings of nouns and adjectives emphasized. About 10 minutes.

(3) Introduce lines 38-61 from book, using map in book or wall map to illustrate. Call attention to the marginal note *multī ↔ paucī,* ad stress *nōn* in answers to *num*-questions (referring to the marginal note opposite lines 49-51). 15 minutes.

(4) Class fills in Exercitium 5 and starts on Exercitium 6.

Assignment: Exercitium 6. Review lines 38-61

Lesson 4

(1) Students correct homework (Exercitium 6) from overhead transparency. *Note:* This is a time-saving device for in-class correction. About 5 minutes.

(2) Students answer questions on the whole chapter, including questions introduced by *num* and *quid* (Exercitium 7). 7-10 minutes.

(3) Teacher instructs students, in Latin and English, to close books and listen. Teacher introduces *Litterae et numerī* (lines 62-83) by writing single letters and numbers, giving Latin utterances related to them in the text. Take paragraph by paragraph, modeling orally for student imitation. Mix recitation pattern — full choral, part choral, individual. Students are then instructed to open books and read text aloud, by individuals. If student has difficulties, teacher supplies model for full choral repetition first, then repetition by individual student. About 15 minutes.

(4) Review 62-83 by rapid chain reading. 5 minutes.

(5) Do first two or three sentences from Pensum A and Pensum B, writing them on the blackboard. This is to make sure students know what to do with their assigment.

Assignment: Write Pensum A and Pensum B. Write each Latin sentence in full. Practice reading them aloud.

Lesson 5

(1) Correct Pensum A from overhead projector. 10 minutes.

(2) Introduce *Singulāris et plūrālis* (lines 84-106) from textbook. Flashcards may be used to reinforce the concept og singular and plural, e.g. drawings of an island (*īnsula*) on one side or card and of two or three islands (*īnsulae*) on the reverse. About 7 minutes.

(3) Instruct students to take a piece of scratch paper, setting up two columns headed *Singulāris* and *Plūrālis*. Write words at random on the blackboard. Students are to insert them in the proper columns.

1. *īnsula*	5. *fluviī*	9. *numerus*	13. *īnsulae*
2. *oppidum*	6. *littera*	10. *oppida*	14. *numerī*
3. *vocābula*	7. *vocābulum*	11. *fluvius*	15. *exemplum*
4. *litterae*	8. *ōceanus*	12. *exempla*	16. *imperium*

Correct in class. 10 minutes.

(4) Do Exercitium 8 orally by rapid chain drill. Go on to ask questions from Exercitium 9 or Pensum C, as time permits.

Instead of (3) and/or (4) some teachers may prefer to rehearse COLLOQVIVM PRIMVM in class with different pairs of students taking the parts of *Mārcus* and *Iūlia*. Ask for volunteers to learn the parts by heart.

Announce test for next day.

APPENDIX III: PREFACES TO THE FIRST EDITION OF *LINGVA LATINA PER SE ILLVSTRATA*

Preface by ROBERT SCHILLING, Director of the Latin Institute of the University of Strassburg Director of Studies at the École des hautes études

"Man by instinct tends first towards that which is in conformity with nature." Does not this observation of Cicero[1] also apply to methods of teaching ?

I often recall the statement of Paul Valéry, who once said, in effect : "I shall believe in Latin when I see a young man or girl get into a train and open a volume of Virgil or Horace for pleasure." Let us acknowledge that our high school graduates rarely feel the need for this aristocratic pleasure.

Why ? It would be pointless to dilate again on the different causes of disaffection that seem to weigh irremediably on the future of Latin. The same applies to the vigorous reaction that developed in France with the birth of the *Mouvement pour le latin vivant*, marked by three international conferences, held successively at Avignon in 1956, Lyon in 1959, and Strassburg in 1963.

An obvious truth has become inescapable : the crisis of Latin is *above all* a crisis of method. Our received pedagogy is essentially characterized by the *translation* and *explanation* of texts. Experience has shown that this method, precise and analytic, is nevertheless insufficient to impregnate the minds of young people with the genius of the language, to give them the desire to *read* with an open book. Texts have tended to become a pretext for grammar review rather than remaining the object and purpose of study.

In the face of this degradation, many teachers respond with resignation : "What do you expect ? By the time we get to Livy or Virgil, too many students have forgotten the *rules of grammar* they are supposed to know and are completely ignorant of *vocabulary.* » Thus a sort of vicious circle developed. It was a sterile stagnation : one reviewed the evanescent rules *ad nauseam*, one repeated endlessly words which never anchored themselves in the memory. Instead of offering our students a living mastery of Latin, inviting them to think in accord with the genius of the language, we offered them exercises of dissection on the cadaver of a "dead language." Thus we slid into a decadent scholasticism of philological coloration. What good for our students to learn the laws of morphology or phonetics, if they remained incapable of understanding the verses of Virgil or the prose of Tacitus ?

Let us then bravely cast away the stumbling block of the "dead language" and learn Latin as a living language. This does not mean renouncing the valuable aspects of our classical pedagogy, but rather finally creating the conditions that will make its goals no longer illusory. A student should first of all *feel at ease* in the use of the language, as he feels at ease in his own language, which he has learned in a natural manner. We must return to *nature*.

In this regard, I do not hesitate to praise the immense value of the Danish method developed by Arthur Jensen and applied to Latin by Hans Ørberg. It takes the student, whether a child or an adult beginner, as it were by the hand in proceeding from the simplest phrases to the most complex. The vocabulary is learned *naturally,* by the composition of phrases: each word is repeated a sufficient number of times in different contexts.

The student progressively familiarizes himself with the words and structure of the phrase, without having recourse to translation. Each chapter is followed by an appendix which summarizes grammar and proposes exercises of application. For the convenience of the student, the long vowels have been marked and the marginal notes show the characteristic features of the language and provide explanatory illustrations. The structure of *LINGVA LATINA PER SE ILLVSTRATA* is enriched with happy strokes of inspiration throughout.

The subject of the story, developed in the course of the

book, is a Roman family with three children. The reader is initiated to essential aspects of daily life in Rome by the adventures of this family. He is inculcated with the usages of Roman life, learning also idiomatic words and characteristic expressions. The student of *LINGVA LATINA PER SE ILLVSTRATA* will not stumble over basic questions like "What day is it? May 16," nor will he be brought up short by allusions to the religious, political, or administrative life of ancient Rome. In the second volume, *ROMA AETERNA,* he will become more familiar with Rome, the principal monuments of the *Urbs*, the essential facts of its legend and history. The course kills two birds with one stone, so to speak. At the end of the course the student has been initiated into both the Latin language and the genius of Rome.

A vocabulary of some 3,500 words and a general knowledge of Roman life will then permit him to practice the reading of Livy or Cicero. But that is not all. The student attains these results by a methodical and fecund impregnation based on a natural approach. How many heartbreaks avoided by the child who is no longer repulsed by tiresome grammatical exercises but captivated by the development of a fascinating story! What encouragement for the adult whose circumstances have heretofore prevented him from entering the mysterious world of Latinity!

Behold finally a living method for approaching Latin! To the young studen who has been disappointed by a bad start, as to the adult who wonders whether it's not too late, we would like to repeat the decisive words that St. Augustine heard one day in other circumstances: *"Tolle, lege, tolle, lege!"* Yes, take up and read!

PREFACE
by Dr. SCEVOLA MARIOTTI
Professor of Latin literature and language at the University of Urbino

The introduction of a method of teaching Latin such as that of Hans H. Ørberg should be favored and encouraged.

In one fundamental respect it is superior to the still prevalent methods: in the manner in which it concretely considers the living use of the language as prior to grammatical abstractions. And it is precisely the demand for concreteness that will be appreciated above all in this application to an ancient language, brilliantly successful despite the not minor difficulties of applying a system first developed for the practical teaching of modern languages.

Ørberg provides an introduction to the Latin world. The simple linguistic models that represent the nucleus of each lesson are constructed or chosen in a manner so as to recall, together with objects and experiences characteristic of all places and times, some fundamental aspects of ancient life and civilization. The pleasing illustrations that vary the elegant pages of the work serve this same purpose.

Thus the pages of *FAMILIA ROMANA* make up a small, elementary encyclopedia that will not only interest the youngest students in middle school, but will not seem too infantile for the *sērī studiōrum* who come to Latin later in life. Students in this latter category are for various reasons very few in Italy, but their numbers could increase with the help of a method such as this one.

A warning seems appropriate in presenting the "nature method" in countries where humanist prejudices are deeply rooted.

This approach does not by itself aim at propagating the use of Latin. The frequent occasions for conversation in the *pēnsa* are justified entirely, in the context of a living method of teaching, as means to facilitate first contacts with the ancient language. Latin is not learned in order to be spoken or written. Aside from the customs of religious societies, the use of Latin today is justified only in a certain tradition of philology, or on the rare occasions when the language meets a definite poetic need, as in the work of Pascoli. Otherwise, efforts to bring it to life, aside from being anti-historical, would put in danger, through untold inevitable compromises, the very seriousness of the study of the language. The only reason for learning Latin is direct contact with ancient authors, the experience of a lost world that nevertheless cannot be eliminated from the civilization and culture of our time.

For this reason Ørberg, following Jensen's principles, does not use any language but Latin in his lessons. If the work is based for the most part on a cycle of Latin passages expertly composed by the author, it is nevertheless clear that he is is eager to free himself from this expedient and to leave the talking to the ancients, who are indeed preponderant by the end of the course.

We hope that also in Italy numerous ranks of student-readers will follow him on this journey to the classics.

PREFACE
by Professor Dr. EMILIO SPRINGHETTI S. J.
Professor of the "Schola Superior Litterārum Latīnārum"in the Pontifical Gregorian University of Rome

It may seem bold, in the midst of so many polemics about the life and pedagogy of the Latin language, to present for this language—which some insist on considering dead or half-dead—the most living method yet conceived for learning a living language.

Such is the method introduced some years ago by Arthur M. Jensen for the study of English, judged favorably by eminent professors of linguistics, and crowned with exciting results. The "nature method" as applied by Hans Ørberg is a new, ingenious application of the "direct method": exclusive use of the Latin language; gradual and practical learning of vocabulary and grammatical structures through recourse to easy expressions of thought, varied in all their forms, coordinated and organized in such a way as not only to explain each other reciprocally, but also to shed always more light on the Latin manner of thinking and to convey the means of understanding and expressing oneself in Latin; constant exercise of the memory and intelligence, necessitating on the one hand the constant recollection of words, meanings, and forms, and other hand the intuition of new meanings through suitable illustrations and easy connections; the completion of forms and sentences that, left incomplete in special *pēnsa* joined to each lesson, review and test the solidity of the student's progress.

It is true that this method was developed specifically for students working on their own, whatever their age and level of culture. But it can also be used in the classroom under the guidance of an expert teacher who, while helping the students isolate, collect, and recall forms and meanings, should not take away from the effort the students invest, nor accelerate the course to the detriment of their great advantage, however gradual.

The apparent ease of approach should not lead the student

to suppose that a superficial, cursory or hasty reading is sufficient; the reading should be methodical and serious, because every page is linked to the prior one, which holds the keys to unlock the new difficulties and the light to illuminate new breaks in the horizon. This seamless process continues harmoniously through the whole course.

If one thinks of the teaching of Latin in recent times, there is no doubt that Ørberg's method marks, if not exactly an innovation, a resumption of the treatment of Latin as a living language. It succeeds in conveying, to a certain degree, that linguistic sense that current methods too often fail to give. If carried through with perseverance and seriousness, it will not be an exaggeration to speak of practical results such as already attained for modern languages, and of an initial contribution to a restoration of living Latin augured by the International Congress at Avignon in the September of 1956.

Another advantage of the course is that, with a vocabulary of some 3,500 words, it provides a basis for the immediate direct reading of classical authors. This can be done in the terms of traditional syntax and grammatical study, directed not towards learning the language (as is now done with Latin and foreign languages) but towards the completion and bringing to consciousness of notions that have already been practically assimilated. This complementary traditional theoretical recapitulation and practical contact with the authors will recommend itself to those who want to arrive at the true *mēns Latīna* and the perfect knowledge of the peculiar syntactic and stylistic structure of the language.

Thus understood and applied, this method will greatly contribute to the solution of the debate about methods of Latin teaching, and earn the consideration that it is already receiving in other countries.

Praefatio A.D. LEEMAN in studiorum universitate Amstelodamensi Latinitatis professor

Numquam fere in patria nostra tot artes grammaticae Latinae elucubratae sunt quot hisce temporibus, numquam tamen vera notitia linguae latinae tam pusilla fuit quam hodie; quae res quanto in discrimine sit tota humanitatis disciplina ad oculos demonstrat. Quaerenti mihi quemadmodum huc delapsi simus occurrerunt haec.

Multa per saecula ita didicerunt linguam Latinam discipuli, ut plurimarum regularum scientia nisi latinitatem veterum auctorum intellegere possent. Simul cotidie fere ipsi sermone Latino utebantur, nec solum auctores veteres interpretabantur, sed etiam suo Marte imitabantur. Ita per imitationem linguam latinam quasi vivam colebant et restaurabant. Eruditio autem vere humanistica in hisce duobus constabat: et interpretari posse monumenta vetera, et loqui posse sermone veterum. Quamquam Montaigne ille humanista iam scripserat 'c'est un bel et grand agencement que le grec et latin, mais on l'achète trop cher'

Saeculo XIX in scholis minus temporis impendi poterat studiis humanitatis, qaippe quae cederent aliis studiis, quae magis ad usum vitae pertinere videbantur. Quantum temporis supererat, minus erat quam quod et ad grammaticam discendam et ad auctores legendos et ad imitationem veterum sufficere posset. Ita factum est ut imitatio, quae studia humaniora quasi coronabat et qua lingua Latina vita quadam perpetua fruebatur, omnino tolleretur. Sane grammaticam ediscendo et auctores legendo haud spernendam scientiam linguae Latinae sibi parare et poterant et possunt discipuli; sed postquam ea studia per quinque vel sex vel etiam plures annos assidue culta sunt, etiamtum recte Latine scribere nesciunt, nedum loqui.

Apparet institutionem, qua tantum operae impenditur ad eventum tam mediocrem, imbecilliorem esse quam ut necessitatibus hodiernae vitae resistere possit. Quae cum ita sint, multi homines docti novas rationes docendi humaniora invenire conantur, quibus huic difficultati atque discrimini occurratur. Cotidie fere novae artes grammaticae in lucem prodeunt, neque quisquam bene novit quo se vertat.

Imprimis ratio et via directa quae dicitur quaerentibus se obtulit. Videmus enim infantes notitiam perfectam et absolutam linguae sibi parare nec tamen aut grammaticam perdiscere aut themata facere. Qua in re nimis facile oblivisci solent homines docti mentem adulescentuli vel iuvenis aliquantum differre ab infante. Tantum abest ut ratio ea discendi commodior atque proclivior sit, ut etiam molestior atque operosior saepe sit discipulis, quibus multa varia et diversa sub oculos veniant et quos difficultates plane obruant! Eo accedit, quod infans sane linguam suam sua sponte mirabiliter perdiscit, neque tamen eo ipso eruditior humaniorque fit. Nam homines sua lingua prius loqui quam scribere discunt, et paucissimi tantum monumenta litterarum intellegere discunt.

Ecce hoc temporis discrimine, quo omnis humaniorum institutio periclitatur, discendi ratio apparet, quae naturalis appellatur. Hoc statim dicam me meliorem rationem neque vidisse neque novisse. Praestat enim omnia rationis directae commoda, cum tamen incommodis quae supra memoravi libera est. Perite et ingeniose huius rationis auctores difficultates ordinaverunt, distribuerunt, temperaverunt. Vere dicere possumus auctores utile dulci miscuisse ita ut alterum ab altero distingui non possit.

Hi libri iucundi sunt nec tamen levitate peccant; discipulus quasi ludens rem seriam et gravissimam penitus cognoscit.

Nostro saeculo Latine loqui discere per se ipsum iam mirabile est - neque dubito quin discipulus huius rationis auxilio duobus fere annis eo pervenire possit, sed - quod maius etiam est - eodem temporis spatio legere et intellegere monumenta litterarum veterum et illos fontes sapientiae atque humanitatis discit. Nam usque a primo fasciculo multa cognoscit quae ad vitam Romanam et cultum antiquorum pertinent, quo facilius in fasciculis posterioribus Sallustium, Livium, Ciceronem legat.

Utinam aliquando haec ratio in scholis nostris adhiberi possit! Quantopere ibi et gaudium et profectum discipulorum augere posset!

PRAEFATIO A.D. LEEMAN

in studiorum universitate
Amstelodamensi Latinitatis professor

Numquam fere in patria nostra tot artes grammaticae Latinae elucubratae sunt quot hisce temporibus, numquam tamen vera notitia linguae latinae tam pusilla fuit quam hodie; quae res quanto in discrimine sit tota humanitatis disciplina ad oculos demonstrat. Quaerenti mihi quemadmodum huc delapsi simus occurrerunt haec.

Multa per saecula ita didicerunt linguam Latinam discipuli, ut plurimarum regularum scientia nisi latinitatem veterum auctorum intellegere possent. Simul cotidie fere ipsi sermone Latino utebantur, nec solum auctores veteres interpretabantur, sed etiam suo Marte imitabantur. Ita per imitationem linguam latinam quasi vivam colebant et restaurabant. Eruditio autem vere humanistica in hisce duobus constabat: et interpretari posse monumenta vetera, et loqui posse sermone veterum. Quamquam Montaigne ille humanista iam scripserat 'c'est un bel et grand agencement que le grec et latin, mais on l'achète trop cher'

Saeculo XIX in scholis minus temporis impendi poterat studiis humanitatis, qaippe quae cederent aliis studiis, quae magis ad usum vitae pertinere videbantur. Quantum temporis supererat, minus erat quam quod et ad grammaticam discendam et ad auctores legendos et ad imitationem veterum sufficere posset. Ita factum est ut imitatio, quae studia humaniora quasi coronabat et qua lingua Latina vita quadam perpetua fruebatur, omnino tolleretur. Sane grammaticam ediscendo et auctores legendo haud spernendam scientiam linguae Latinae sibi parare et poterant et possunt discipuli; sed postquam ea studia per quinque vel sex vel etiam plures annos assidue culta sunt, etiamtum recte Latine scribere nesciunt, nedum loqui.

Apparet institutionem, qua tantum operae impenditur ad eventum tam mediocrem, imbecilliorem esse quam ut necessitatibus hodiernae vitae resistere possit. Quae cum ita sint, multi homines docti novas rationes docendi humaniora invenire conantur, quibus huic difficultati atque discrimini occurratur. Cotidie fere novae artes grammaticae in lucem prodeunt, neque quisquam bene novit quo se vertat.

Imprimis ratio et via directa quae dicitur quaerentibus se obtulit. Videmus enim infantes notitiam perfectam et absolutam linguae sibi parare nec tamen aut grammaticam perdiscere aut themata facere. Qua in re nimis facile oblivisci solent homines docti mentem adulescentuli vel iuvenis aliquantum differre ab infante. Tantum abest ut ratio ea discendi commodior atque proclivior sit, ut etiam molestior atque operosior saepe sit discipulis, quibus multa varia et diversa sub oculos veniant et quos difficultates plane obruant! Eo accedit, quod infans sane linguam suam sua sponte mirabiliter perdiscit, neque tamen eo ipso eruditior humaniorque fit. Nam homines sua lingua prius loqui quam scribere discunt, et paucissimi tantum monumenta litterarum intellegere discunt.

Ecce hoc temporis discrimine, quo omnis humaniorum institutio periclitatur, discendi ratio apparet, quae naturalis appellatur. Hoc statim dicam me meliorem rationem neque vidisse neque novisse. Praestat enim omnia rationis directae commoda, cum tamen incommodis quae supra memoravi libera est. Perite et ingeniose huius rationis auctores difficultates ordinaverunt, distribuerunt, temperaverunt. Vere dicere possumus auctores utile dulci miscuisse ita ut alterum ab altero distingui non possit.

Hi libri iucundi sunt nec tamen levitate peccant; discipulus quasi ludens rem seriam et gravissimam penitus cognoscit.

Nostro saeculo Latine loqui discere per se ipsum iam mirabile est - neque dubito quin discipulus huius rationis auxilio duobus fere annis eo pervenire possit, sed - quod maius etiam est - eodem temporis spatio legere et intellegere monumenta litterarum veterum et illos fontes sapientiae atque humanitatis discit. Nam usque a primo fasciculo multa cognoscit quae ad vitam Romanam et cultum antiquorum pertinent, quo facilius in fasciculis posterioribus Sallustium, Livium, Ciceronem legat.

Utinam aliquando haec ratio in scholis nostris adhiberi possit! Quantopere ibi et gaudium et profectum discipulorum augere posset!

PRAEFATIO DAG NORBERG IN STUDIORUM
UNIVERSITATE HOLMIENSI PROFESSOR

Saeculum vicesimum magnis et mirabilibus rebus insignitum est quas viri scientiarum et artium technicarum periti effecerunt. Novas inventiones paene cotidie audimus, et automatio quae vocatur, vis atomica ad usum hominum adhibita, exploratio earum cosmicarum regionum quae extra orbem terrae sitae sunt aliaque his similia fortasse spem nobis iniciunt novam aetatem venire et magnum saeculorum ordinem de qua vates cecinit ab integro nasci. Quibus consideratis credere possis veteres artes liberales et in primis studia antiquitatis classicae scientiis et artibus technicis cedere debere. Sed longe aliter res se habet. Quo longius enim ars technica progreditur, eo magis iis nobis litteris studendum est quibus ad veram humanitatem fingimur. Alioquin periculum est - ut technici ipsi recte viderunt - ne homunculi machinis serviant, ne pecudum ritu inconstanter vitam miserriman degant, licet copiae per machinas augeantur. Quin etiam ipse progressus artis technicae periclitabitur, nisi eundem laborem eandemque operam humanitati et liberalibus artibus dederimus.

At studium humanitatis non plane idem est quod studium litterarum antiquarum. Concedo id quidem. Sed hic cultus vitae ad quem populi Occidentis deducti sunt e studio litterarum Graecarum et Romanarum profectus est. Hodieque necesse est res e fonte repetere et initia et progressus humani cultus et ordinem rerum gestarum cognoscere, si praesens tempus prorsus intellegere volemus. Constat exempli gratia Platonem ad doctrinam Christianorum formandam plurimum valuisse, constat sapientiam et disciplinam medii aevi ex Aristotele et e iuris consultis Latinis pendere, constat litteras recentioris aetatis theatro et fabulis Graecorum et Romanorum incredibile quantum debere. Quod antiqui cogitando et fingendo invenerunt, quasi fundamentum quoddam est totius huius cultus quo nunc utimur. Adhuc philosophi, auctores, artifices saepissime divino instinctu Musarum Graecarum et Latinarum fruuntur. Quod magno nobis documento est ne putemus cultum antiquum mortuum nisi ad memoriam annalium non pertinere: adhuc spirat, adhuc fructus uberes profert. Si humanitatem antiquorum, qui nihil humanum a se alienum putabant, recte intellexerimus, pertinaciter atque inepte contra nostri temporis inventa non contendemus, sed virtute ac viribus humanis confisi eundem spiritum tradere possumus quo olim, temporibus veterum Graecorum et Romanorum et post mille quingentos fere annos cum veteres artes renatae sunt, viri summo ingenio praediti et artis peritissimi tot et tanta effecerunt, ut quasi novus ordo rerum oriretur.

Accedit quod populi Occidentis studio humanitatis antiquae artissime inter se coniuncti sunt. Nam initiis consideratis penitus discere possumus qualis sit natura nostri cultus, quibus ex elementis compositus sit quantoque cum labore constructus sit. Fieri non potest quin id opus summae nobie curae sit quod tanto temporis impendio aedificatum est et ad quod nihil quod quidem aliquid valet gratis accessit. Populi divisi si patrimonium commune acceperint, communitatem amissam recuperabunt. Studium litterarum Graecarum et Latinarum quippe cua populorum Occidentis commune sit, fundamentum societatis multo stabilius est quam quod ex usu earundem machinarum efficitur.

Humanitatem veterem a libris veteribus in linguas nostrae aetatis conversis et ex libris manualibus et ex commentationibus diversi generis aliqua ex parte cognoscere licet. Sed ex ipsis fontibus potionem vitalem haurire non possumus nisi linguae operam dederimus. Haud parvi est laboris Latine discere; nam ea de lingua in primis agitur, ut nunc sunt res in Occidente. Multi ardore quodam amoris huic se studio dedissent, nisi difficultatibus quae tironibus occurrunt et ratione abstrusa et spinosa qua plerumque grammatica docetur deterriti essent. Itaque maximo cum gaudio opus quod "LINGVA LATINA PER SE ILLVSTRATA" inscribitur a viro doctissimo Hans H. Ørberg, adiuvante Arthur M. Jensen, editum accepinus, quo novam viam aperuit qua ad litteras Latinas cognoscendas itur. Quae via quantam utilitatem nobis afferat, disserte ab aliis explicatum est. Hic satis est pauca dixisse. Vel ex titulo apparet discipulos per "naturae rationem" novam linguam eodem fere modo memoriae mandare quo iis patrius sermo natus est. Iam inde ab initio nulla alia lingua nisi Latina utuntur; nihil in linguam recentiorem convertitur. Quid novae voces significent e contextu apparet, et totiens repetuntur ut memoriae infigantur. Sic copia verborum Latinorum sensim augetur, multo quidem facilius et multo certius quam si verba separata e glossario aliquo discas. Sua observatione et sua comparatione dlscipuli etiam grammaticam pedetemptim e contextu verborum percipiunt. Etiamsi antequam incipiunt nihil e grammaticorum scientia cognitum habeant, ad linguam Latinam hac via discendam venire possunt. Nam ad grammatcae quoque cognitionem quasi natura ipsa ducente sine ambagibus praescriptorum abstrusorum veniunt, dummodo textum attento animo legant.

Insigne ac notabile est "naturae rationem" ad eam linguam discendam adhibitam esse quae mortua appellatur quia nemini iam innata viva voce traditur. Id eo fieri potuit quod auctor huius operis Romam antiquam et omnes res ut tunc erant optime cognovit. Animo suspenso narrationem sequimur quae ab initio uno tenore fluit et qua comperimus, quomodo Romani domi et in civitate vitam cotidianam et festam vixerint. Studio huius operis absoluto non solum usus linguae. bene partus est sed etiam cognitio haud contemnenda cum aliarum rerum Romanarum tum vitae communis, historiae, religionis. Suavissime et facillime liberis studiis ea via inceditur qua "Lingua Latina" ad id quod propositum est deducit, scilicet ad ea sine difficultate legenda quae Cicero, Livius aliique nobiles Latini scripserunt et posteritati tradiderunt.

PRAEFATIO IACOBI DEVOTO
IN STUDIORUM UNIVERSITATE FLORENTINA
GLOTTOLOGIAE PROFESSOR

'Naturae Ratio' ad linguam Latinam docendam accommodata, quae, ut est simplex et perfecta, iam apud exteras nationes valde probata est, non propriis tantum virtutibus Italis commendatur. Ea autem, quae L. Hjelmslev.praefatus est editioni in usum Danorum prolatae, ad omnes cuiusvis linguae lectores pertinent.

Sed nobis illustrandas esse censeo causas externas et adventicias quae, praeter intimas virtutes, 'Naturae Rationis' gravitatem videntur potissimum apud nos augere. Ac primum quidem considerandum est quam multi Italorum Latine discant in omnibus fere scholarum gradibus; si igitur aptiore ratione ac via linguam Latinam tironibus tradere coeperimus, hoc discipulorum multitudini maiori usui erit apud nos quam apud ceteras gentes. Deinde, si institutio linguae Latinae cum recentiorum linguaruin institutione adaequatur secundum 'Naturae Rationem', omni

compage, ut ita dicam, traditae grammaticae sublata, universa grammaticae doctrina penitus commutatur.

Nemo enim ignorat grammaticam explicationem Italici sermonis in nostris scholis plerumque praeteriri, cum omnis cura et intentio in verbis excutiendis describendis digerendis Latinitatis tantum docendae causa adhibeatur; quod ipsius Latinitatis cognitioni est detrimento. Nam vetus et communis opinio est declinationes, casus, voces medias, consecutionem temporum, sententias pendentes pro gerundiis nostris non sine tarditate usurpatas non modo ut scriptores legi et cognosci possint discenda esse, sed etiam ut discipulorum ingenia, velut ictu quodam pulsa atque agitata, nova hac exercitatione excolantur.

'Naturae Ratione' adhibita cum aditus ad veteres scriptores expeditior fiat, quaestiones quas attigi ita dirimuntur ut investigatio artis grammaticae cum studio patrii sermonis rursus coniungatur; atque utinam illa ab hoc numquam esset seiuncta. Quod si lectores ad scriptores Latinos facilius accedunt, tum animi contentio, qua grammatica discitur, prorsus non detrahitur, sed alio transfertur. Quin etiam dixerim 'Naturae Ratione' ea fundamenta iaci ut institutio de grammatica, cum studio patrii sermonis rursus coniuncta, vim suam non solum servet sed etiam augeat. Haec enim institutio non est quasi quoddam plumbeum onus quod ipsum per se mentes repleat vel aliquid certius et uberius praebeat, sed facultas ratione concipiendi ac penitus intellegendi id quod natura attingimus et intuemur.

Duo alia inde manant eaque Italis utilia: nam et grammaticae institutio ad nostri sermonis studium translata accuratior, subtilior, vigens denique fiet, cum omnes discipuli, minimi quoque natu, assidue neque operose linguam ipsi pariant suis quisque necessitatibus aptam, et qui Latine didicerint naturae normam potius quam artis praecepta sequentes, ii Ciceroniane scribere vana animi oblectatione fortasse neglegent, at certe sentient se viam ingressos esse quam munitissimam etiam ad Latinam linguam recte et ratione intellegendam. Ita contentio illa memoriae, que in elementis grammaticae perdiscendis nunc carere non possumus, in mentis delectationem convertetur cum linguae ordo et ratio et structura, adiuvante natura iam perceptae, mente penitus cognoscantur

Quaedam vero omittam quae hoc quidem loco levioris momenti videntur: num sit Latine aetate nostra loquendum, de qua re nuper in quodam doctorum hominum congressu actum est, aut num Latino sermone, utique in commodiorem formam redacto, viros technicos omnium nationum uti par sit.

Sed 'Naturae Ratione' hoc praesertim efficitur, ut multo faciliora prima elementa fiant. Quam rationem non ignoramus inventam esse non ad scholarum discipulos erudiendos, sed ad instituendos per litteras eos omnes qui parvo labore cum humanitatis historiaeque disciplinis tum Latinis litteris domi studeant. Sed apud nos Latine in scholis praecipue discitur; quare facere non potui quin dicerem quantopere linguae Latinae institutio, 'Naturae Ratione' adhibita, et facilior fieret et immutaretur. Neque tamen putandum est 'Naturae Rationis' vim ita deformari, sed potius eam extra cancellos egressam esse quibus inventores eam incluserant.

Quae cum maximi sint momenti, restat ut breviter tantum percurramus alia quaedam quae viri docti, hos libellos legentes, statim probabunt et laudabunt: syllabas longas et breves, novam rem et insolitam tironibus, diligenter signatas, paginas et typos accurate dispositos, verba inter se contraria ut 'bonum malum' saepenumero coniuncta, lentum sed firmum progressum ex sententiis facilioribus, quae peropportune bis terque repetuntur, ad narratiunculas, ad T. Livii, Ciceronis, aliorum denique locos. Nam in extrema huius Operis parte scriptorum Latinorum integros locos invenimus; quos cum discipuli nullo negotio intellegent, tum se tam perfecte eruditos esse mirabuntur.

Si quis forte miratur 'Naturae Rationem' apud Danos et ortam et statim prospera fortuna usam esse, is Daniam meminerit non solum grammaticae generalis, quae dicitur, inventricem, sed etiam patriam fuisse O. Jespersen doctissimi viri, in Anglorum lingua explananda et interpretanda principis; ibi autem maxime pro incolarum numero linguae et grammaticae studia vigere et complures viros hac arte perdoctos summa auctoritate floruisse. Ex dono quod nunc inde accipiunt utinam Itali quam laetissimos fructus ferant.

APPENDIX IV: ESSENTIAL BIBLIOGRAPHY ON ASPECTS OF ROMAN CIVILIZATION

LINGUA LATINA PER SE ILLUSTRATA offers many points of departure for developing the presentation of aspects of ancient Roman civilization. The study of the language is integrated throughout with study of social and material aspects of the culture which produced it. An understanding of the Roman world is in any case necessary for a full comprehension of the language itself. By the same token, it is impossible to gain an accurate sense for the Roman world while remaining ignorant of its language. Thus the *LINGUA LATINA* course, albeit primarily a language course, also becomes an instrument through which students can easily have access not only to classical culture *strictō sēnsū*, but to western culture in the larger sense.

The books mentioned in this bibliography are for the most part not written for adolescents; in working with younger students the instructor will want to extract from these books whatever materials may be useful. Any suggestions for adding to this bibliography are welcome.

Here is a list of some subjects which may be developed on the basis of chapters in *FAMILIA ROMANA*:

the Roman empire
the *familia*
slavery in the ancient world
the *vīlla*
Roman roads
Commerce
Pastoral life
Medicine
Roman proper names: the *tria nōmina*
The army and military life
The calendar and the divisions of time
Schools in Greece and Rome
Navigation
Numbers and letters
The status of women
Domestic life
icursus pūblicus and private *tabellāriī*
Greco-Roman culture
Greek and Roman mythology
Agriculture
Banquets and *symposia*
The Roman fleet
Gladiators and *lūdī circēnsēs*

GENERAL WORKS

Hornblower, Simon and A. Spawforth, eds. 2003. *The Oxford Classical Dictionary.* New York: Oxford University Press

Paoli, Ugo Enrico. 1975. *Rome: Its People, Life, and Customs.* R.D. Macnaghten, trans. Westport Conn: Greenwood Press.

Dupont, Florence. 1993. *Daily Life in Ancient Rome.* Christopher Woodall, trans. Cambridge, Mass.: Blackwell

Casson, Lionel. 1998. *Everyday Life in Ancient Rome.* Baltimore: Johns Hopkins.

Carcopino, Jérôme. 1968. *Daily Life in Ancient Rome : The People and the City at the Height of the Empire.* H.T. Rowell, ed, E.O. Lorimer, trans. New Haven: Yale University Press.

Ariès, Philippe and Georges Duby, eds. 1987-1991. *A History of Private Life. Vol. I: From Pagan Rome to Byzantium.* (Paul Veyne, ed.) Cambridge, Mass. : Belknap Press of Harvard University Press

Wacher, John, ed. 1987. *The Roman World.* New York: Routledge.

Giardina, Andrea, ed. 1993. *The Romans.* Lydia G. Cochrane, trans. Chicago : University of Chicago Press.

Koller, Herman. 1983. *Orbis pictus Latinus : vocabularius imaginibus illustratus.* Zürich : Artemis Verlag.

Seyffert, Oskar. 1961. *A Dictionary of Classical Antiquities.* Revised and edited by Henry Nettleship and J. E. Sandys. New York: World Publishing.

WORKS ON SPECIFIC SUBJECTS

Bonner, Stanley F. 1977. *Education in Ancient Rome.* Berkeley: University of California Press.

Bowen, James. 1972. *A History of Western Education.* London: Methuen.

Marrou, H.I. 1982. *A History of Education in Antiquity.* G. Lamb, trans. Madison, WI: University of Wisconsin Press.

White, K.D. 1970. *Roman Farming.* London: Thames and Hudson.

Percival, J. 1976. *The Roman Villa.* London: B. T. Batsford.

Hodge, P. 1975. *The Roman House.* London: Longman.

Hopkins, K. 1978. *Conquerors and Slaves.* Cambridge: Cambridge University Press.

Finley, M.I. 1980. *Ancient Slavery and Modern Ideology.* London : Chatto & Windus.

Finley, M.I. ed. 1968. *Slavery in Classical Antiquity.* New York: Barnes and Noble.

Davies, R.W. 1989. *Service in the Roman Army.* New York: Columbia University Press.

Gabba, Emilio. 1976. *Republican Rome, the Army, and the Allies.* P.J. Cuff, trans. Berkeley : University of California Press

Rosenstein, N.R. 2004. *Rome at War.* Chapel Hill : University of North Carolina Press.

Wilkes, J. 1972. *The Roman Army.* Cambridge: Cambridge University Press.

Brunt, P.A. 1982. *Social Conflicts in the Roman Republic.* London: Chatto and Windus.

Ormerord, H.A. 1987. *Piracy in the Ancient World.* New York: Dorset Press.

Bickerman, E.J. 1980. *Chronology of the Ancient World.* London: Thames and Hudson.

Rawson, Beryl, ed. 1986. *The Family in Ancient Rome.* Ithaca, NY: Cornell.

Starr, Chester G. 1975. *The Roman Imperial Navy, 31 B.C.--A.D. 324.* Westport, Conn. : Greenwood Press

Scarborough, John. 1969. *Roman Medicine.* Ithaca, NY: Cornell.

Kajanto, I. 1965. *The Latin cognōmina.* Rome: G. Bretschneider.

APPENDIX V:
LATINITAS: THE MISDIAGNOSIS OF LATIN'S RIGOR MORTIS [22]

By Prof. Terence O. Tunberg, University of Kentucky

When mention is made of the Latin language, the first things which spring to mind for most people are toga-clad individuals bustling around in the forum, legions, eagles, gladiators—in a word, the ancient Romans, and an ancient, long-gone language.

But the use of Latin, a thing which in fact most Latin teachers seem to regard as incidental and not really their concern, persisted long after the passing of the ancient world in which it first developed, unlike the languages of the Hittites, Babylonians and many other ancient peoples. Indeed it is fair to say that Latin is not merely an ancient language; of the bulk of extant literature written in Latin, the antique portion is by far the smallest[23]. Latin writing and all genres of Latin literature flourished widely not in the Middle Ages alone but even up to comparatively recent times. The use of the language has persisted in some quarters even in the twentieth century.

Yet teacher and professors of Latin in schools and universities tend to teach the language as though it were only ancient and Roman, and nothing after the Roman empire, or even the early Roman empire, was written in Latin that is worth reading as Latin. Has anyone ever heard of a university department of French, for example, in which all literature in the French language written after the reign of Louis XIV is excluded from the standard curriculum? Why then is the Latin tradition treated this way?

To be fair and accurate, we should note that this situation doesn't apply equally to all regions today where Latin is taught. In Spain and Scandinavia, to name two important cases, mediaeval Latin and Neo-Latin studies are actively cultivated in departments of classical languages, at least at the university level. In most areas, however, particularly in the English speaking world, the situation is very different. Latin is usually reduced to the study of the Romans, and not rarely to something even less than that. Indeed in some traditional British university classical language departments, Christian authors like Tertullian and Jerome are not even taught: Christian Latin is regarded as belonging in the department of Divinity.

I invite readers to consider what we might gain by working towards changing this situation. Of course I do not advocate removing Roman authors from the typical repertoire of student reading. But I do assert that the mediaeval and modern periods of Latin should also be represented, in the form of selected texts, on standard high school as well as university curricula everywhere. From the very beginning of the process of learning Latin, students should be made aware of its entire history. Students at every level should have some contact with more recent works in Latin, not merely the ancient ones. They should acquire some notion of how vast and complex is this later Latin tradition and what a fundamental part of our intellectual heritage is contained within it and handed down by it.

Against this view, some may perhaps assert that in these later periods Latin was nobody's native language. Every Roman, by contrast, had Latin as the maternal tongue. In the Roman period, Latin was associated with one primary set of institutions. For these and other reasons, the Latin language cannot be studied apart from the culture of the ancient Romans, and this is why the way of teaching Latin in England and the United States has evolved the way it has over the last two centuries. The classical Latin authors with which our Latin training should be concerned are Romans, preferably pagan, and no others.

To anyone advancing this point of view, we may advance several responses. First, the proposals advanced here do not imply that the study of Roman culture and its accompanying classroom activities be entirely removed from Latin studies, but rather that some information about the development of later western ideas, institutions, and movements (as contained in Latin writings) be added to Latin teaching across the board, a point to which we shall return later.

Secondly, we ought to keep in mind that Latin was not the first language of everyone who wrote in Latin during the Roman empire. Can we assume that provincial authors such as Columella, Apuleius, Tertullian, and Augustine heard their earliest words in the cradle from nurses who spoke Latin? In the case of at least two late imperial Latin authors, Ammianus and Claudianus, we know that Latin was not their native tongue. Yet none of these authors, in university programs at least, is absolutely excluded from the list of those whom more advanced students might sometimes read (even if they don't appear in high school curricula). And indeed, if we may compare another literary discipline, are we accustomed to exclude from the English curriculum such authors as Conrad and Nabokov, for whom English was not at all a native language?

We might in fact take the view that precisely because in the post-Roman period Latin was no one's native tongue, but rather a common lingua franca of Europe's educated, whatever their vernacular speech, and that Latin became the language reserved for expression of the most advanced and sophisticated thoughts, while never losing a less formal, 'spontaneous,' and convivial strain, this phase of Latin is especially worthy of the attention of Latin students. Anyone who studies Laitn should have some exposure to the ages when Latin was the acquired language of almost every educated person and Latin literature flourished as the vehicle not only for theology, philosophy, and science, but also poetry, letters, satire, fiction, and many other genres. This is a remarkable phenomenon and a fundamental element in the

22 Reprinted from the ACL Newsletter (Winter, 2000) by the kind permission of the author and the American Classical League.

23 The best comprehensive introductions and guides to the wealth of post-antique material in Latin are F.A.C. Mantello and A.G. Rigg, edd. *Mediaeval Latin. An Introduction and Bibliographical Guide.* (Washington, D.C. 1996); J. Ijsewijn, *Companion to Neo-Latin Studies, Part I. History and Diffusion of Neo-Latin Literature.* Second entirely rewritten edition. Supplementa Humanistica Lovaniensia V (Louvain, 1990); J. Ijsewijn with D. Sacré, *Companion to Neo-Latin Studies, Part II. Literary, Linguistic, Philological and Editorial Questions.* Second entirely rewritten edition. Supplementa Humanistica Lovanensia XIV (Louvain, 1998).

intellectual tradition of Europe and its offshoots.

But, some readers will certainly respond, high school curricula are so often tied to state and national contests and exams, all of which revolve around Vergil, Ovid, Catullus, and Cicero, along with Roman culture and Graeco-Roman mythology. How is it practical to alter that? And where are the editions of mediaeval and Neo-Latin texts suitable for the use of teachers?

Answers to such questions are not lacking. Would it create a catastrophic upheaval to modify the existing curricula and Latin exams, not by removing the Roman material, not by eliminating elements of ancient culture,[24] but by dealing with them more selectively and adding fundamental selections and cultural material from the sectors of mediaeval and early modern Latin? Surely not.

But what about editions appropriate for the classroom? Indeed both anthologies and editions exist. And new editions adequate for school use appear every year. Some of these texts are so well equipped with introductions and notes that teachers need to consult hardly any other sources. And if more doctoral candidates in Latin literature, instead of writing yet more theses about Vergil or Cicero, would produce useful editions of Neo-Latin texts, especially with teachers in mind, teachers might have an even wider and more rapidly growing body of material from which to select. Obviously the emphasis on scholarship in universities can ultimately have an effect on how Latin is taught in schools, and so a word or two about Latin in academic scholarship will not be out of place.

Clearly, it can be important for historians, professors of the national languages such as French or English, philosophers, or theologians to study mediaeval Latin or Neo-Latin texts on occasion. Not rarely such scholars may find themselves dealing with material entirely or largely written in Latin, in fact reading considerably larger quantities of Latin than their colleagues in classics departments, and without translations or commentaries. As a result, a few professors in these disciplines have become excellent Latinists. But, to speak generally, though we find highly competent Latinists now and then in such disciplines (much as some professors of eighteenth-century French, for example, might also, because of

their research orientation, be highly skilled in Italian), and though Neo-Latin scholarship in general has a huge potential to contribute to most humanities with a focus on mediaeval and modern Europe, none of these disciplines revolves principally on the study of post-antique Latin per se—and reasonably so, since none of these disciplines, not even theology or philosophy (in which most of the material may be Latin), was created for the purpose of studying Latin letters as such. Although mediaeval Latin is sometimes offered in classical language departments in the American universities, this is far from routine. The situation is even worse for the study of Neo-Latin literature, which has no departmental basis at all in the typical American or British university. Surely there is something paradoxical about this state of affairs. The study of that linguistic and literary tradition which contains nothing less than the foundations of western thought, a study which deeply affects a wide variety of other humanities disciplines, has no primary place in our universities but is nearly always subsidiary and, in theory, to be studied not on its own merits but for the sake of something else. Surely the mediaeval and more recent end of the Latin tradition is an area to be consistently adopted by departments of Latin or classical languages. Who are better equipped to teach Neo-Latin texts as Latin and in the tradition of Latin writing than professors of Latin? Classical language departments as they now exist would be better named "departments of ancient history," or "departments of ancient studies." We suggest here that any department which rightly claims to teach classical languages and literatures (in which "classical" is understood as Latin and Greek), should, in theory, give equal attention to all phases of the history of Latin literature, namely all periods in which Latin was important and the vehicle for significant writings (and the same may be said for classical or Koine Greek).

What advantages might arise from a general adoption of this wider approach to the Latin tradition in middle schools, high schools, and universities?

First, those of us with an interest in spoken Latin, even if they do this only for pedagogical purposes, will find the wider approach to Latin studies congenial to what they are doing. Probably not a few classicists and teachers (though in smaller numbers now than a few years earlier) regard enthusiasts for oral Latin as members of a kind of "society for creative anachronism" or as extremists trying to revive something extinct for millennia. But such a perspective ignores the long and centrally important tradition, maintained virtually uninterrupted from antiquity, of people who used Latin to express contemporary experience long after Latin ceased to be anyone's vernacular—a tradition that extends in some geographic regions and in some academic fields down to the nineteenth century, or down to our own time if we consider the use of Latin in the Roman Catholic Church. If more of us could get used to thinking of Latin as not merely an ancient phenomenon, such people might find the idea of speaking and writing in Latin in our time much less outlandish.

Secondly, Latin instruction in high schools is often defended on the ground that it provides an excellent window for students into the foundations of western culture. As a result, a lot of diverse non-language material pertaining to Graeco-Roman art,

---

24 For teachers interested in finding an anthology of mediaeval Latin, I can especially recommend *Reading Mediaeval Latin* by Keith Sidwell (Cambridge, 1995). To find other anthologies and editions, one should first consult the general works mentioned in note 2. In addition the *Journal of Medieval Latin* (published by Brepols in Belgium, but available in major US libraries) reviews each year new editions of mediaeval Latin texts (not all of which are suitable for school use). For new editions of Neo-Latin works, see the annual bibliography found in the back of each issue of *Humanistica Lovaniensia* (published by Louvain University Press, Belgium, but available in major US libraries.) Bryn Mawr Latin Commentaries is a series which includes a number of important mediaeval and Neo-Latin classics. These books are commendable for their very low price, and their extremely extensive commentaries, which help make these texts accessible even to those who are just beginning to read Latin. Also useful for similar reasons are the Toronto Medieval Latin texts, though these editions are equipped with less editorial help than the Bryn Mawr series.

architecture, institutions, society, etc., finds its way into the Latin classroom. But how much richer would be the cultural content of Latin education, if, from the sources of Latin writings, students might learn not just about the Romans and ancient history, but about subsequent western history and civilization—a later phase of the Latin tradition no less important than the Roman era. In the international language of Latin we meet the thoughts of those who shaped our scientific, ideological, and even literary traditions. Those Latin writers were not a group of obscure reactionaries, sequestered from the main lines of creativity in later European culture, but rather the leading minds of mediaeval and early modern west: Abelard, Aquinas, Petrarch, Erasmus, Thomas More, Copernicus, Bodin, Newton, to name a very few. Latin study, moreover, can show how their thought developed on Latin linguistic foundations and how the Roman language, carrying with it Roman ideas, was adapted, and in some cases developed and gave shape to concepts expressed in Neo-Latin. Teachers of Latin possess a vast treasury of material to make their courses richer and more interesting—sadly, a treasure which many ignore.

Latin, teachers say, helps students build vocabulary and verbal skills in English and modern languages. In this respect too we can see the potential for gain from including more recent material. In addition to the basic vocabulary of ancient Latin that continues in use through the Middle Ages and the Renaissance, the special terminology of mediaeval philosophy and various sciences during the Renaissance made a significant contribution to concepts in English and other national languages that would not easily be apparent to those who concern themselves only with ancient texts. The vocabulary of our universities themselves, to name one small example, is a heritage of mediaeval Latin: words like faculty, graduate, bachelor's degree, for instance, are simply anglicized versions of *facultas (atrium, iuris, legum,* etc.), *graduatus, baccalaureatus.*

Adoption of a standard curriculum involving all main periods of Latin could benefit the study of Latin, and indeed all humanities, in universities also. As a result, we would surely see closer ties between classical language faculties and other departments, such as those of history and national languages, in which taking account of mediaeval and Neo-Latin material can be necessary. It is likely that, along with increased cooperation with other departments, the possibilities for winning grants and funding in departments of classical languages would accordingly increase.

In the proposal advanced here lies a potential alleviation of another difficulty commonly encountered by those who run classics courses in universities. How often is it necessary for heads of classics departments to defend to administrators the existence of certain low-enrollment courses? This is especially common in the case of courses at the higher levels involving texts in the original language. If it were customary to include the mediaeval and early modern Latin tradition in survey courses or sequences, and to offer seminars in such authors as well as the usual ancient ones on a regular basis, it is likely that more students in other departments, especially graduate students, would be motivated to participate, and in general Latin studies would extend more widely and attract more adherents.

Finally—and now we come to a question that extends far outside the mundane considerations of enrollment and university structure—it is worthwhile to consider our perspective on the tradition of Latinitas itself. Although in the last 15-20 years interest in Neo-Latin writers and study of their works has increased considerably, particularly in the case of a few major authors, there is still a huge amount to learn about the later phases of Latin literature. No one could doubt that our knowledge of this major patrimony would increase at a considerably enhanced rate if the study of this field were an established element in every Latin department and regularly treated as part of the history of a classical language. As noted above, there is a vast number of interesting texts, some of which have great importance, which should be made generally available in modern, well-annotated editions. What more ideal area for doctoral dissertations in Latin studies? In short, everyone stands to gain, learners, teachers, and researchers, if the same attention is given to the philological study of the recent part of the Latin tradition that has already been given to its beginnings for a long time.

A widening of Latin studies along the lines described here will obviously not happen overnight. Many teachers and professors of classical languages are perfectly happy with the exclusively Graeco-Roman focus of their profession which they learned when they were trained. But others, who gain exposure to the later tradition, will be excited by the actual breadth and richness of the language and literary tradition to which they can have access. Change will happen with teachers. It is up to innovators in the classroom to show their students into the different territories where Latin leads. Inspired by this knowledge, and curious to learn more, students themselves will advance with a new concept of what Latin is and new expectations about what it should mean to us. But it is up to teachers individually to realize the potential that exists.

A version of this paper was presented at the meeting of the Indiana Foreign Language Teachers Association in Indianapolis on Nov. 6, 1999. The author is especially grateful to the Indiana Latin teachers who attended the lecture for their stimulating questions and useful suggestions.

---

25   On these words, see R. Hoven, *Lexique de la prose latine de la renaissance* (Leiden, 1994), or J. F. Niermeyer, Mediae Latinitatis lexicon minus, 2nd edition (Leiden, 1984).

APPENDIX VI

THE FIFTY MOST FREQUENT LATIN VERBS

Compiled by James J. Hessinger on the basis of an analysis of texts from ten Latin authors (five prose authors and five poets, with the proportion of the samples 3:1::prose:poetry). These frequencies are consistent with the analysis of a larger sample in D.D. Gardner, 1971, "Frequency Dictionary of Latin Words," Stanford University Ph.D. dissertation.

© James J. Hessinger. Reprinted by the kind permission of the compiler.

1. sum, esse, fuī, futūrum
2. dō, dare (-dere), dedī (-didi), datum (ditum)
3. ferō, ferre, tulī, lātum
4. eo, īre, iī/ivī, itum
5. faciō (-ficiō), facere (-ficere), fēcī, factum (-fectum)
6. mittō, mittere, mīsī, missum
7. capiō (-cipiō), capere (-cipere), cēpī, captum (-ceptum)
8. videō, vidēre, vīdī, vīsum
9. dīcō, dīcere, dīxī, dictum
10. possum, posse, potuī
11. habeō (-hibeō), habēre (-hibēre), habuī, habitum (-hibitum)
12. veniō, venīre, vēnī, ventum
13. agō (-igō), agere (-igere), ēgī, actum
14. pōno, pōnere, posuī, positum
15. cēdō, cēdere, cessī, cessum
16. teneo (-tineō), tenēre (-tinēre), tenuī (-tinuī), tentum
17. dūco, dūcere, dūxī, ductum
18. stō, stāre, stetī, statum
19. legō (-ligō), legere (-ligere), lēgī, lectum
20. vertō, vertere, vertī, versum
21. petō, petere, petīvī, petitum
22. volō, velle, voluī
23. noscō, noscere, nōvī, nōtum
24. sequor, sequī, secutum
25. moveō, movēre, mōvī, mōtum
26. tendō, tendere, tetendī, tensum
27. scrībō, scrībere, scrīpsī, scriptum
28. vocō, vocāre, vocāvī, vocātum
29. iaciō, iacere, iēcī, iactum
30. relinquō, relinquere, relīquī, relictum
31. quaerō, quaerere, quaesīvī, quaesītum
32. rapiō, rapere, rapuī, raptum
33. cadō, cadere, cecidī, casūrum
34. perio/pereo, perīre, periī/perīvī, peritum
35. fugiō, fugere, fūgī, fugitum
36. parō, parāre, parāvī, paratum
37. vincō, vincere, vīcī, victum
38. –spiciō, -spiciō, -spexī, -spectum
39. putō, putāre, putāvī, putātum
40. iubeō, iubēre, iussī, iussum
41. gerō, gerere, gessī, gestum
42. audiō, audīre, audīvī, audītum
43. crēdō, crēdere, crēdidī, crēditum
44. premō, premere, pressī, pressum
45. pellō, pellere, pepulī/pulsī, pulsum
46. fundō, fundere, fūdī, fūsum
47. statuō, statuere, statuī, statūtum
48. solvō, solvere, solvī, solūtum
49. spectō, spectāre, spectāvī, spectātum
50. currō, currere, cucurrī, cursum

The forms in parentheses above are the forms that appear whenever a preposition or preverb is attached to the verb. Below are the spelling changes possible in the preverbs themselves:

ab-	a-, au-, abs-
ad-	af-, ap-
cum-	co-, con-, com-, col-
ex-	e-, ef-, el-
in-	im-, il-
ob-	oc-, op-, of-, os-
trans-	tra-
sub-	sup-, suf-, sus-
re-	red-
per-	pel-

APPENDIX VII
CATALOGUE OF LATIN SYNTAX

(the Roman numerals refer to chapters in *SYNTAXIS LATINA*, the Arabic numbers to the paragraphs)

This index gives examples of some of the most important syntactic phenomena. Memorizing these examples may be a more effective means of memorizing grammatical rules than starting with the abstract formulation.

I   Cāsus Nōminātīvus

1. Subject of finite verb (subiectum)

Sāpiēns rēs adversās nōn timet.

2. Double nominative/double accusative(nōminātīvus/ accūsātīvus duplex):

Cicerō cōnsul ēlēctus est.

Rōmānī Cicerōnem cōnsulem ēlēgērunt.

3. Vidērī--personal construction (cōnstrūctiō persōnālis)::

Iūlius mihi vidētur pater sevērus esse.

4. Vidērī--impersonal construction (cōnstrūctiō impersōnālis):

Magistrō necessārium esse vidētur tabellārium mittere ad Iūlium.

Discipulīs nōn vidēbātur magistrum recitantem interrogāre.

Iūliō vidētur Mārcum paenitēre pigritiae suae.

Dāvō vidēbātur fore (futūrum esse) ut Mēdus fugeret.

5. Dīcitur, nārrātur, trāditur, fertur, etc.:

Daedalus labyrinthum aedificāvisse nārrātur.

Trāditum est Ariadnam fīlum Thēseō dedisse.

II   Cāsus Accūsātīvus

1. Direct object (obiectum dīrēctum)

Rōmulus urbem Rōmam condidit.

Mēns regit corpus.

2. Verba iubendī, sinendī, et prohibendī cum accūsātīvō et īnfīnītīvō:

Iūlius servum saccum portāre iubet.

Dāvus iubētur crumēnam suam pōnere in mēnsā.

Aemilia iānuam claudī iussit.

3. Impersonal verbs (verba impersōnālia: pudet, miseret, taedet, piget, paenitet):

Puerum pudet factī suī.

Mē paenitet dīxisse hoc.

Mē pudet hoc ā fīliō meō factum esse.

Mē paenitet quod tē offendī.

4. decet, dēdecet, fallit, fugit, latet, praeterit, iuvat:

Tē decet honestē vīvere.

Puellās decet verēcundia.

Mē fugit nōmen illīus.

Mē fugit quod nōmen eī sit.

Mē iuvat Latīnē discere.

Mē iuvat *LINGVA LATINA PER SE ILLVSTRATA* .

Mē fallit memoria.

5. Double accusative (accūsātīvus duplex/accūsātīvus geminus):

Doceō discipulōs grammaticam.

Cēlō mātrem vēritātem.

Poscō sociōs frūmentum.

Flāgitō rēgem senātum / ā senātū.

Rōmānī Cicerōnem cōnsulem ēlēgērunt.

6. Verba petendī et interrogandī:

Aemilia Quīntum interrogat.

Pāstor Iūlium ōrat.

Senātōrēs rogāvērunt cōnsulem sententiam.

Petō ā tē librum.

Quaerō ex tē vēritātem.

7. Transitive Latin verbs that are intransitive in English (e.g. dēspērāre)

Dēspērāre pācem/dēspērāre dē pāce.

8. Verba affectuum (dolēre, flēre, lūgēre, rīdēre, horrēre, querī, mīrārī):

Mārcus Iūliam rīdet.

Antōnius flet / lūget patrem mortuum.

Quīntus horret medicum.

9. Olēre, redolēre, sapere, resipere, sitīre:

Sitiō honōrēs.

Haec sententia sapit Cicerōnem.

10. Compound verbs with the accusative (verba composita cum praepositiōnibus quibus plerumque adiungitur accūsātīvus):

Circumīre īnsulam.

Illum hominem / ad illum hominem adiī.

11. Cognate or internal accusative (accūsātīvus cognātae sīgnificātiōnis):

Pugnāre pugnam.

Vīvere vītam.

12. Accusative of respect/Greek accusative (accūsātīvus graecus/ relātiōnis/ dāterminātiōnis):

Nūdus pedem.

13. Accusative of extent of space (accūsātīvus spatiī):

Vāllum decem pedēs altum.

Via centum pedēs lāta.

Fossa decem pedum.

14. Distance constructions (accūsātīvus aut ablātīvus cum verbīs temporālibus 'abesse' et 'distāre'):

Urbs distāns trium mīlium passuum spatiō.

Hadrūmetum abest ā Zamā trecenta mīlia passuum.

15. Age constructions (constructiones quae ad aetatem pertinent):

Mārcus octō annōs nātus est.

Mārcus nōnum annum agit.

Mārcus est puer octō annōrum.

Mārcus octō annōs habet.

16. Accusative of exclamation (accūsātīvus exclāmātīvus) :

    Beātōs agricolās!

    Bene Antōnium!

17. Adverbial accusative (accūsātīvus adverbialis):

    Māgnam, māximam partem.

    Librī id genus. (= liber huius generis)

    Hostēs partim occīsī, partim captī sunt.

    Verba tua multum mē commovent.

III. Cāsus genetīvus

1. Subjective genitive (including the genitive of possession) and objective genitive (genetīvus subjectīvus, genetīvus possessīvus, genetīvus obiectīvus):

    Amor mātris.

    Domus rēgis = domus rēgia.

    Timor mortis.

2. Partitive genitive (genetīvus partitīvus):

    Paulum aquae.

    Plūs pecūniae.

    Parum cibī.

    Multum vīnī.

    Ūnus discipulōrum.

    Ūnus ex discipulīs.

    Quid novī?

    Aliquid novī.

    Satis pecūniae.

    Nēmō vestrum.

    Nihil malī.

    Nihil malum.

    Nihil turpe.

3. Genitive of quality (genetīvus quālitātis/genetīvus dēscriptiōnis):

    Vir summae sapientiae.

    Vir summā sapientiā.

    Vir brevī statūrā.

4. Predicate genitive with the genitives of possession or quality (genetīvus praedicātīvus)

    Haec domus est patris meī.

    Mātris est līberōs cūrāre.

    Meum est id facere.

5. Genitive of price and of value (genetīvus pretiī et aestimātiōnis):

    Quantī stat?

    Māgnō stat.

    Decem sēstertiīs stat.

    Māgnī aestimāre.

    Parvī aestimāre.

Parī pretiō.

Decem sēstertiīs aestimāre.

Prō nihilō facere.

Māgnī mōmentī esse.

Floccī nōn facere.

6. Genitive of the charge (genetīvus crīminis):

    Accūsāre fūrtī.

7. Genitive of the penalty (genetīvus poenae):

    Morte damnāre.

    Capite / capitis damnāre.

8. Genitive of memory (genetīvus memoriae):

    Meminisse illīus reī / illam rem.

    Oblīvīscī illīus reī / illam rem.

    Meminisse illīus hominis.

    Oblīvīscī illīus hominis.

9. Constructions with interest and rēfert:

    Iūliī interest agrōs invīsere.

    Meā interest/rēfert linguam Latīnam discere.

    Tuā interest/rēfert linguam Latīnam discere.

    Eius interest/rēfert linguam Latīnam discere.

IV Cāsus datīvus

1. Dative of indirect object (obiectum indirectum)

    Mittō tibi epistulam.

    Dō eī librum.

2. Dative of possessor (datīvus possesīvus):

    Mihi est liber.

    Mihi nōmen est Iūlius / Iūliō.

3. Dative of personal interest: datīvus ēnergicus et datīvus commodī / incommodī):

    In cōnspectum vēnerat hostibus.

    Nihil difficile est amantī.

    Nōn vītae, sed scholae discimus.

    Deō nostra altāria fūmant.

    Sī quid peccat mihi peccat.

4. Ethical dative—confined to personal pronouns (datīvus ēthicus)

    Quid mihi Celsus agit?

    Ecce tibi Sēbōsus!

5. Dative of reference (datīvus iudicāntis):

    Ut mihi dēfōrmis, sīc tibi māgnificus.

    Quīntia fōrmōsa est multīs.

    Nāvigantibus Prochytam, mōns Mīsēnus est ad dextram.

6. Dative of purpose/double dative (datīvus fīnālis):

    Diem colloquiō statuere.

    Hoc est mihi cordī.

    Dōnō tibi dō hunc librum.

    Auxiliō vēnērunt Iūliō.

7. Dative of agent (datīvus agentis):

Omnibus patria amanda est.

8. Dative with special verbs (verba quibus plerumque adiungitur datīvus):

Tibi assentior.

Tibi grātulor.

Tibi cōnfīdō.

Mihi persuāsit.

Ignōsce mihi!

Lesbia Catullō nōn nūpsit.

Multī dīvitibus invident.

Eī persuādēre nōn potuī.

Parce mihi!

Linguae Latīnae libenter studēmus.

Dīvitibus invidētur.

9. Constructions with dōnāre, circúmdare, exuere, induere, aspergere, etc.:

Dōnō tibi librum.

Dōnō tē librō.

Induō tē veste.

Induō tibi vestem.

10. Verbs with different constructions and senses (constructiōnēs diversae):

Cavē canem!

Cavē canī!

Sextus litterīs vacāre solet.

Ab officiīs vacāre.

11. Dative with compound verbs (verba composita cum praepositiōnibus quibus plerumque adiungitur datīvus):

Librōs addere bibliothēcae / ad bibliothēcam.

12. Verbs of excellence (verba praestantiae):

Cicerō omnēs / omnibus praestat ēloquentiā.

Cicerō omnēs superat ēloquentiā.

V. Cāsus ablātīvus

1. Construction with opus est:

Properāre / properātō opus est.

Nummīs mihi opus est.

Nummī mihi opus sunt.

2. Ablative of material (ablātīvus māteriae):

Ānulus ex aurō / aureus.

3. Ablative of comparison (ablātīvus comparatīvus):

Melior sum frātre / quam frāter.

Mihi is doctior vidētur quam tibi.

Mālō esse quam vidērī bonus.

Amīcus ille, quō nēmō mihi cārior est.

4. Ablative of means (ablātīvus īnstrūmentālis/īnstrūmenti):

Equō vehī.

Per tabellārium aliquid dē mē sciēs.

5. Ablative with special deponents: ūtī, fruī, fungī, vescī,

potīrī:

Agricola arātrō ūtitur.

Carne vescī.

Iugurtha Numidiā / Numidiae potītur.

Rērum potīrī.

6. Ablative of respect/specification (ablātīvus limitātionis/respectūs/relātiōnis):

Mārcus et Sextus differēbant mōribus.

7. Constructions of dīgnus and indīgnus:

Dīgnus laude.

Dīgnus quī laudētur.

8. Ablative of argument (ablātīvus argūmentī):

Dē amīcitiā disputāre.

Liber dē amīcitiā.

9. Ablative of separation and abundance (ablātīvus sēparātīvus et abundantiae):

Carēre pecūniā.

Egēre auxiliō.

Implēre aquā.

Plēnus nummōrum.

Refertus nummīs.

VI. Time constructions (locūtiōnēs temporālēs)

1. Quandō? Ablative of time when or within which (ablātīvus temporis)

Kalendīs Iānuāriīs.

Hōrā nōnā.

Aestāte.

Annō quadrāgēsimō quārtō ante Chrīstum nātum Caesar necātus est.

In bellō.

Bellō Iugurthīnō.

Sub fīnem diēī.

Circā illum annum.

2. Quō temporis spatiō? Intrā quod tempus?

Decem diēbus.

Intrā decem diēs.

3. Quō temporis intervāllō?

Quīntō quōque annō lūdī Olympiī celebrābantur.

4. Quotiēs in temporis spatiō?

Semel in annō.

5. Quantō ante? Quantō post?

Decem annīs ante.

Ante decem annōs.

Decem ante annīs.

Decem ante annōs.

6. Quamdiū?

Per decem annōs.

Decem annōs.

7. Ex quō tempore?

Tertium iam annum.

Tot annōs.

Decem abhinc annōs.

Ante (hōs) quīnque annōs.

8. Post quod tempus?

Post ūnum annum.

9. In quod tempus?

In posterum!

Ūsque ad mortem.

VII. Place constructions (locūtiōnēs locālēs)

1. Ubi?

In Italiā.

Rōmae.

Athēnīs.

Neāpolī.

2. Quō?

In / ad Italiam.

Rōmam.

Athēnās.

Neāpolim.

3. Unde?

Ab urbe venīre.

Ē patriā ēgredī.

Dē caelō dēscendere.

Rōmā.

Athēnīs.

Neāpolī.

4. Quā?

Per Rōmam.

Ībam forte viā Sacrā.

VIII. Negative pronouns, adjectives, and adverbs:

nēmō, nihil, nūllus etc. post particulās ' et' aut 'ut' fīnālēs

Et nēmō → nec quisquam

Et nūllus → nec ūllus

Et nihil → nec quicquam

Et numquam → nec umquam

Et nusquam → nec usquam

Ut nēmō → nē quis

Ut nūllus → nē ūllus

Ut nihil → nē quid

Ut numquam → nē umquam

Ut nusquam → nē usquam

IX Intransitive use of the passive

Ūrit silvam.

Silva ūritur.

Augeō amōrem meum.

Amor meus augētur.

Minuō mercēdem.

Mercēs minuitur.

Mūtō rem.

Rēs mūtātur.

Pāscō ovēs.

Ovēs pascuntur.

Sānō aegrōtum.

Aegrōtus sānātur.

X. Modus indicātīvus

1. Latin indicative in place of English subjunctive with certain verbs and idioms (indicātīvus pro coniūnctīvo):

Dēbēmus festināre.

Longum est omnia explicāre.

Numquam putāveram.

2. Latin indicative for English subjunctive with pronouns, adjectives, and adverbs that are reduplicated or composed with -cumque, or with the disjunctive particles sīve... sīve/seu...seu (indicatīvus pro coniūnctīvo):

Quisquis / quīcumque est ille...

Sīve hoc vērum (est) sīve falsum est...

3. Temporal priority (tempus antecēdēns--cōnsecūtiō temporum modī indicātīvī):

Cum pervēnerō Rōmam vidēbō amphitheatrum Flavium.

XI. Modus coniūnctīvus

1. Hortatory subjunctive (coniūnctīvus hortātīvus) :

Bonum vīnum bibāmus!

2. Potential subjunctive (coniūnctīvus potentiālis):

Quid dīcam?

Quid dīcerem?

Aliquis dīxerit.

3. Optative subjunctive (coniūnctīvus optātīvus):

Utinam veniās!

Utinam vēnerit!

Utinam venīret!

Utinam vēnisset!

4. Concessive subjunctive (coniūnctīvus concessīvus):

Dīcat sānē hoc Mārcus: tamen nōn crēdō.

XII. Negative imperative (prohibitiō):

Nōlī hoc facere!

Nōlīte hoc facere!

Nē hoc fēceris!

Nē hoc faciās!

XIII. Infinītīvus

1. Accusative with infinitive (accūsātīvus cum infinītīvō/ ōrātiō obliqua):

Dīcō 'tē bonum puerum esse.'

Tē advēnisse gaudeō.

Gaudeō quod advēnistī.

2. Complementary infinitive (infinītivus complētīvus)

Dīcere solēbat.

Oblīvīscī nōn possum quae volō.

XIV. Participia

1. Participle with verbs of perception (cum verbīs sentiendī):

Videō Mārcum scrībentem.

Videō Mārcum scrībere.

2. Linked participle (participium coniūnctum):

Hostēs urbem captam incendērunt.

3. Ablative absolute (ablātīvus absolūtus):

Mortuō Caesare.

Omnibus spectantibus.

Caesar, hortātus mīlitēs, commīsit proelium.

XV. Gerundium et gerundīvum

1. Gerund and gerundive (gerundium et gerundīvum):

Mihi legendus est liber.

Dēsīderium legendī librōs.

Dēsīderium legendōrum librōrum.

2. Periphrastic construction (periphrasis/constructio periphrastica):

Moritūrus sum!

Omnibus moriendum est.

XVI. Supine (supīnum):

Veniō tē salūtātum.

Difficile dictū.

XVII Sequence of tenses with the subjunctive (cōnsecūtiō temporum modī coniūnctīvī)

Nesciō quid Mārcus agat (nunc)

Nesciō quid Mārcus ēgerit (herī)

Nesciō quid Mārcus āctūrus sit (crās)

Nesciēbam quid Mārcus ageret (tunc)

Nesciēbam quid Mārcus ēgisset (anteā)

Nesciēbam quid Mārcus āctūrus esset (posteā)

XVIII. The use of suī, sibi, sē and suus, sua, suum:

Iūlius loquitur cum Cornēliō et cum frātre suō (= Iūliī).

Iūlius loquitur cum Cornēliō et cum frātre eius (= Cornēliī).

Paulus effēcit ut omnēs sibi crēderent.

Factum est ut nēmō eī crēderet.

XIX. Subjunctive in subordinate clauses and modal attraction (Coniūnctīvus in enūntiātīs subordinātīs et attractiō modī vel modālis):

Putō eum esse virum quī tē adiuvāre possit.

Sī vīveret pater tuus, hoc nōn probāret.

Sī quis tē interroget, eī vērum dīc.

XX. Interrogātīva

1. Direct interrogatives (interrogātīva recta):

Ubi est Rōma?

Est-ne Rōma in Italiā?

Num Rōma in Graeciā est?

Nōnne Rōma in Italiā est?

Utrum hoc vērum est an falsum?

Vērumne est hoc an falsum?

Vērum est hoc an falsum?

2. Indirect interrogatives (interrogātīva obliqua):

Nesciō utrum hoc vērum sit an falsum.

Nesciō vērumne sit hoc an falsum.

Nesciō vērum sit hoc an falsum.

XXI. Substantive clauses with quod (ēnūntiāta substantīva particulā 'quod' inducente):

Bene facis quod linguae Latīnae studēs.

Tē laudō quod linguae Latīnae studēs.

Gaudeō quod linguae Latīnae studēs.

XXII. Substantive clauses with ut (ēnūntiāta substantīva quae ā particulā ' ut' incohantur):

Bone Deus, fac ut vīvat!

Tē hortor ut linguae Latīnae studeās.

Tē rogō ut linguae Latīnae studeās.

Cūrā ut valeās.

XXIII. Substantive clauses with quīn (ēnūntiāta fīnālia particulā 'quīn' inducente):

1. Nōn dubitō quīn:

Nōn dubitō quīn rēs ita sē habeant.

2. Verba impediendī et recūsandī:

Prohibeō quōminus id faciās.

Prohibeō nē ē cubiculō exeās.

Nōn prohibeō quīn Rōmam eās.

Nōn prohibeō quōminus illum librum legās.

XXIV. Fear clauses (verba timendī):

Timeō nē hostēs adveniant.

Timeō nē nōn discam bene linguam Latīnam.

Timeō ut pecūniam māgnam accipiam.

XXV. Purpose clauses (ēnūntiāta fīnālia):

Studeō / studēbō ut discam.

Studēbam / studuī / studueram ut discerem.

XXVI. Result clauses (ēnūntiāta cōnsecūtīva):

Tam bonus est ut omnēs eum ament.

Tam bonus erat ut omnēs eum amārent.

Hic saccus maior est quam ut ā puerō portārī possit.

XXVII. Causal clauses (ēnūntiāta causālia):

Eum amō quod bonus est.

Dīcit sē eum amāre quod bonus sit.

XXVIII. Temporal clauses (ēnūntiāta temporālia):

Cum prīmum eum vīdit, (eum) amplexus est.

Ubi prīmum eum vīdit, (eum) amplexus est.

Ut prīmum eum vīdit, (eum) amplexus est.

Simul ac (atque) eum vīdit, (eum) amplexus est.

Postquam eum vīdit, (eum) amplexus est.

Titus iānuam pulsat antequam intrat.

Studē antequam magister tē interroget.

Dum Rōmae cōnsulitur, Saguntum expugnāta est.

Dum spīrō, spērō.

XXIX.   Concessive clauses (ēnūntiāta concessīva):

Etsī doctus est, historiam nātūrālem tamen ignōrat.

Tametsī doctus est, historiam nātūrālem tamen ignōrat.

Quamquam doctus est, historiam nātūrālem tamen ignōrat.

Quamvīs doctus sit, homō omnia scīre nōn potest.

Etiamsī omnēs eum reprehendant, vir probus semper honestē agit.

Licet mē reprehendant omnēs, dīcam quid sentiam.

XXX. Relative clauses (ēnūntiāta relatīva):

Quā sapientiā es.

Quae tua sapientia est.

XXXI. Comparative clauses (ēnūntiāta comparātīva)

1. Simple comparative clauses (ēnūntiāta comparātīva simplicia) :

Ut homō vīvit, ita moritur.

Antōnius tam bonus est quam Paulus fuit.

Idem sentiō atque tū.

2. Hypothetical comparative clauses (ēnūntiāta comparātīva irreālia):

Quasi stultus sim omnīnō, sīc mē alloqueris.

Tamquam stultus sim omnīnō, sīc mē alloqueris.

XXXII.   Conditional sentences (sententiae condiciōnālēs reālēs, possibilēs, irreālēs):

Sī hoc dīcis, errās.

Sī hoc dīcās, errēs.

Sī hoc dīcerēs, errārēs.

XXXIII. Conditional clauses (ēnūntiāta condiciōnalia):

Ōderint, dum metuant.

Sextus potest sē dēfendere, dummodo cum singulīs certet.

APPENDIX VIII: SYNOPSIS VERBI LATINI

PERSONA:_____ NUMERUS:_____

PARTES PRINCIPALES:_____

VOX ACTIVA   VOX PASSIVA

MODUS INFINITIVUS

PRAESENS_____

PERFECTUM_____

FUTURUM_____

MODUS INDICATIVUS

PRAESENS_____

IMPERFECTUM _____

FUTURUM_____

PERFECTUM_____

PLUSQUAMPERFECTUM_____

FUTURUM PERFECTUM _____

MODUS CONIUNCTIVUS

PRAESENS_____

IMPERFECTUM _____

PERFECTUM_____

PLUSQUAMPERFECTUM_____

MODUS IMPERATIVUS: PRAESENS

SINGULARIS_____

PLURALIS _____

MODUS IMPERATIVUS: FUTURUM

SINGULARIS_____

PLURALIS _____

PARTICIPIA

PRAESENS_____XXXXXXXXXXXXXXXXXX

FUTURUM_____